Contemporary Indian Dramatists: Critical Perspective

Dr.M. Ananthi Devaraj

Published by

BONFRING®
Intellectual Integrity

Contemporary Indian Dramatists: Critical Perspective

9 789386 176134 >

ISBN 978-93-86176-13-4

₹ 250

Author

Dr.M. Ananthi Devaraj

Bonfring
309, 2nd Floor, 5th Street Extension, Gandhipuram,
Coimbatore-641 012.
Tamilnadu, India.
E-mail: info@bonfring.org | Website: www.bonfring.org
Phone: 0422-4213231

Dedicated to

My Parents

Preface

India had its own systematic and elaborative drama even before two thousand years. Indian drama nestled in the cradle of classical Sanskrit dramas, and it can be classified into two groups: Sanskrit drama and Prakrit drama in vernacular language. After the decline of classical Sanskrit drama, Indian dramas registered a substantial development in the regional languages of India. Despite the foreign invasions and political changes, they persisted to exist as the potent tool of entertainment and enlightment.

There were many dramatists who had tried their hands at writing plays. As a matter of fact, most Indian English plays are translated works. Some of them by writers themselves, while some by others. A very few plays are originally written in English. The stunted journey of Indian English play is attributed to many factors.

One of them is non-availability of stage worthy plays. Writing and staging of the plays are two different tasks. In the same way, viewing the play and reading the play are quite two different experiences. Reading a play renders more information and less excitement, whereas viewing a play is the most exciting, appealing and memorable thing.

Indian English Drama is growing slowly and steadily for carving its niche in its realm of commonwealth literature. Since the pre-independence era, there have been constant efforts to create the plays with due dramatic qualities. Even after decades together, the attempts were not met with handsome result.

The origin of Indian drama in English can be traced back to the pre-independence era. Krishna Mohan Banerjee wrote the first Indian English play entitled *The Persecuted or Dramatic Scenes Illustrative of the Present State of Hindoo Society in Calcutta.* It appeared in 1831 on the literary horizon. Thus, the journey of Indian English Drama embarked with the appearance of this play more than a country before the independence era.

The tradition of Indian English Drama has been enriched and augmented further in the post–independence epoch. Gradually, it began to develop as a powerful form for the creative expression. The marked difference between Pre and Post Independence drama is that most of the dramas were written in verse during pre-independence era, whereas the postcolonial dramatists showed much inclination to prosaic drama.

1. INTRODUCTION

Drama has been a very influential and powerful medium in the English literature because of its audiovisual medium of expression. Drama is a mimetic representation of life combining in itself the real and the fictional, art and reality and representing the events and characters within a dimension of space and time. It combines the qualities of narrative poetry with those of visual arts. It is a narrative made visible.

The history of dramatic activity goes far back, beyond historical or literary records, and virtually every culture in every period has produced spectacles of one kind or another. The tradition of European Drama began with the ancient Greeks about twenty-five hundred years ago. Spectacles and all kinds of performances were produced in many Greek cities, but drama developed in Athens. The theatre of ancient Greece evolved from religious rites which date back to at least 1200 B.C.

Musical performances and dramatic recitations both were part of the four religious festivals associated with the annual grape harvest held between December and March. The festivals honoured Dionysus, the god of wine and revelry. Beginning in the sixth century B.C., three of the festivals featured public competitions in drama but the most important of them was the City Dionysia held for about five days in the late March or early April.

For many years, the festival included several days of dithyramb contests—competitions involving hymns or narrative lyric sung by a large chorus. This was followed by the main competition between dramatists, who were sponsored by wealthy individuals. Each playwright produced a trilogy of tragedies and one satyr play over a period of three days.

The three tragedies focused on a single subject or on unrelated subject while the satyr play ordinarily consisted of a farce on an erotic subject and Dionysian theme, with actors costumed as satyrs, half man and half goat. By the sixth century B.C., a masked actor was introduced into the dithyrambs. This actor would engage in a dialogue with chorus, and this can validly be seen as birth of theatre. This innovation is credited to Thespis, a priest of Dionysus, a playwright as well as a poet. According to a Greek chronicle of 3rd century B.C., Thespis was also the first winner of a theatrical award.

Tragedy and comedy are two kinds of drama that we find in Greek period. Aeschylus was the first dramatist to use two characters and turned dithyramb into drama. He added second actor (antagonist) to interact with the first and introduced props and scenery and reduced the chorus from fifty to twelve. In his plays, he makes a point, echoed by historians, dramatists and psychologists: that the root of evil and suffering is usually human arrogance.

Aeschylus plays that have survived are *The Suppliants, The Persians, The Seven Against Thebes* and *Prometheus Bound*, and his crowning work is the *Orestia*, a trilogy of tragedies (*Agamemnon*, *The Libation Bearers* and *The Eumenides*) first performed in 458 B.C. Thematically, the trilogy talks of excessive human pride, arrogance or hubris and investigates the effects of a curse from one generation to the next.

Sophocles introduced the third actor in Greek drama and stressed on drama between humans rather than between the humans and gods. His most famous plays that have survived are *Ajax*, *Trachiniae*, *Electra*, *Philoctetes*, *Oedipus Rex*, *Oedipus at Colonus* and *Antigone*. His plays are full of irony and are about the folly of arrogance and the wisdom of accepting fate.

Antigone explores the meaning and limits of a citizen's duty of obedience to law and authority and of the Athenian's oath of allegiance. The responsibilities of leaders, military and political, to those whom they lead, are as much a theme of *Ajax* or *Oedipus the King* as of *Seven against Thebes* or *The Persians.* According to Sommer stein, Sophocles plays do not normally bear any direct relation to specific contemporary events, but in a broader sense most of them are highly relevant to the public concerns of a polis community.

Euripides was another dramatic talent to emerge on scene in Athens. His repertoire includes *Medea, The Children of Heracles, The Trojan Women, Ion, The Bacchae* etc. However, Euripide's plays were not about gods or royalty but provided place for peasants alongside princes. He showed the reality of war, criticized religion and portrayed the forgotten of society: women, slaves and the old.

The historical development of the comedy is not as well recorded as that of tragedy. Greek comedy had two periods: Old Comedy represented by Cratinus and Aristophanes, and New Comedy', whose main exponent was Menander. Although middle period also existed but the middle comedy is largely lost, i.e. preserved only in relatively short fragments in authors such as Athenaeus of Naucratis. As no complete middle comic plays have been preserved, it is impossible to offer any real assessment of their literary value. In ‗Old Comedy'period, Aristophanes is the sole important figure who is worthwhile to be mentioned.

His plays that have survived are *The Acharnians, The Knights, The Wasps, Lysistrata, The Clouds, Women at the Thesmophoria, The Frogs* and *Wealth* etc. In his plays, Aristophanes ridiculed the gods, Athenian institutions, popular and powerful individuals, and we also find in them the mistaken identities, ironic situations, ordinary characters and wit.

Aristophanes lampooned the most important personalities and institutions of his day, as can be seen, for example, in his buffoonish portrayal of Socrates in *The Clouds*, and in sexual and political farce *Lysistrata. Lysistrata* openly challenges Athenian social codes that prevented women from participation in government, leveling political criticism-however hilarious-at the governors of Athens.

Menander is regarded as the representative of New Comedy'. His plays are *The Shield, The Curmudgeon, The Arbitration, Hated, Shorn, The Girl from Samos* and *The Sicyonian*. The crucial plot elements of Menandrian comedy are love, deception and discovery. For the first time love became a principal element in the drama.

Nearly always many of the characters are kept ignorant of vital facts, either through circumstances or through the machinations of others, and much of the action springs from such machinations; the truth is generally known to the audience and its discovery by the characters tends to be a climactic moment in the action.

In the middle ages, the roman theatre came under the control of Roman Catholic Church. In theatre liturgical dramas were performed by priests and church members in churches and monasteries. There were three types of dramas: Mystery or Cycle plays, Miracle plays and Morality plays. Mystery plays were sanctioned by church, but produced by guilds. They portrayed the cycle of Christian history from the creation of the world until the last judgment.

Miracle plays dramatized the lives, the conversions, the miracles, and sometimes the martyrdom of saints. The most famous and influential of them are the morality plays, which flourished from the fourteenth century through sixteenth century. These plays taught a lesson through allegorical characters representing vices or virtues.

The drama of the period was relatively free to respond to social issues and concerns of the age, inspired rather than hampered by the tradition. Religious and political issues were not allowed to be the subject-matter of the drama. Despite such regulation, the theatre could not have survived without the support of the court. In the mid-1570s some companies like Kings Men got approval from authorities and public theatres began to be built and licensed in London.

Plays were performed in public and private theatres and at the court. Shakespeare's writing career acts as a convenient register of how fashion changed. Before 1600, he wrote history plays on English subjects, such as Richard II and Henry IV and on Roman subjects, such as Julius Ceaser. He also wrote romantic comedies, including *A Midsummer Night's Dream* and *As You Like it*, at this time. He then wrote his successful tragedies-*Hamlet, Othello, King Lear* and *Macbeth*. His comedies were concerned with serious moral and social problems. Towards the end of his career, he wrote romances such as *The Winter's Tale* and *The Tempest*, plays dealing with forgiveness and hope.

Marlowe was the first great dramatic celebrant of the aspiring mind of Renaissance man and it is this renaissance spirit-desire to comprehend and dominate the universe-which gets reflected in *Doctor Faustus*. In overall conception and in certain structural details, Marlowe's *Doctor Faustus* is greatly influenced by English morality play tradition. Faustus is a moral child whose crucial act-signing of the bond-invites his damnation while simultaneously it begins the painful process of his moral and emotional education.

In *Doctor Faustus,* Marlowe charts a collision course between the comforting certainties of the medieval world and the anxieties of the modern world. Faustus is torn between these alternatives and his tragedy is, to an extent, the tragedy of the age in which he lives. The intensity with which Marlowe scrutinizes his protagonist's divided mind gave impetus to the greatest tragedies of the Elizabethan period.

Like *Dr. Faustus,* Shakespeare's tragedies concentrated on the inner moral life of the protagonist, its growth or debasement which connects it with the Christian world view. However, Shakespeare suppresses, to the benefit of his tragedies, explicit theological references.

Similarly, evil is more humanized in Shakespeare, being diffused through and embodied in more naturalistically conceived characters. His greatest strength is his characterization.

In his tragedies, we witness the destruction or waste of human fineness and this loss is connected with the spread of evil spilling outwards like a deadly poison from some single act of folly and feeding on everything that comes in its way. This evil is later destroyed but this is no cause for rejoicing since the good and the innocent have been destroyed too.

Shakespeare also wrote comedies highlighting issues like the irrationality of love, social value of love and marriage. Ben Johnson's kind of comedy is different from Shakespeare's both in method and effect. In the prologue to *Every Man in His Humour* (1598), Ben Jonson claimed that his comedies were essentially realistic-that we would find in them deeds and language such as men do use.

Some of Ben Jonson's writing seems to be a thinly veiled attack on Shakespearean comedy because it is romantic-romantic in the sense that it employs strange, wondrous, essentially non-realistic materials. It is not easy to call Shakespeare Romantic and Ben-Jonson realistic. Ben-Jonson's characterization is fantastic, distorted and extravagant as can be seen easily by thinking of characters in *Volpone* (1606) or of Sir Epicure in the *Alchemist* (1610).

The crucial distinction between Shakespeare and Ben Jonson lies not in the degrees of relative realism but in the fact that Jonson's comedy is satiric and that its aim is to hold folly to overt ridicule. In spirit and techniques, his work resembles the classical writers of antiquity who insisted on the corrective function of comedy than the medieval romance tradition which influenced Shakespeare.

Ben Jonson laid emphasis on the idea that comedy should be —accommodated to the correction of manners which had been put forward by the Roman orator Cicero. The effect is very different from the sense of the festive celebration and ceremonious reconciliation in Shakespearean comedy. Some critics feel that many of Ben Jonson's plays, and especially *Volpone,* can hardly be called comic at all. *Volpone* is a universal satire on man's greed and gullibility. The venation setting enables him to mount a devastating attack on the materialism of renaissance Europe and the resemblances between the play's world and acquisitive modern society need no stressing elaboration.

In latter developments in comedy, Moliere is one the world's great comic masters. His plays like *Tartuffe* (1664), *The Misanthrope* (1660), *The Affected Ladies* (1659) and *The Bourgeois Gentleman* (1670) expose the hypocrisy and lust, the hyper-refinement of fashionable partisans, their over-elaborate manners and grotesquely convoluted polite conversation.

His plays do not often judge from absolute norms of religion and morality, but from more relative social standards. His aim is to correct and improve the manners of society, by reducing affectation rather than lashing vice. For instance, Dorine, the maid of the household in *Tartuffe*, her spirit and commonsense, as well as her role in the play, relate her clearly to the witty slave of the Roman comedy of Plautus and Terence, and show Moliere‘s instinctive awareness of ancient comic traditions.

Tartuffe‘s concentration on serious vice and in the monstrosity of the central figure resembles Jonson's *Volpone*. However, Moliere‘s play is at once less extreme than Jonson‘s and yet more somber. Jonson exaggerates his types of greed and credulity to fantastic degrees so that despite the deep moral thrust of *Volpone*, we are made to share in the dramatist‘s enjoyment of and relish for the world he has created. However, the pervasive value of Moliere‘s dramas is that of good sense, the pursuit of the golden mean.

As Philinte in *The Misanthrope* says, -True reason lies in shunning all extremes. His comedy makes fun of those follies which are a threat to the structure of the society as that society may be conceived of by a rational man who did not expect human beings to be perfect. His masterpiece, *The Misanthrope*, dramatizes the conflict between a man's attempt to sustain his individual integrity and the compromises forced on him by the dictates of the social living.

With the restoration of Charles II to the throne of England in 1660, theatres were reopened after eighteen years. Restoration comedies concern themselves, like Moliere‘s, with social manners, but with a crucial narrowing of range and tone. The plays audiences were comprised of gallants, men-about town, courtiers and people of fashion who were hostile to the values of the bourgeoisie and citizenry which they saw unstylish and dominated by a repugnant puritan earnestness.

Restoration Comedy is realistic in that it reflects a real society, even if that society lacks any depth. The plays of George Etherege illustrate most of the above generalizations. However, it is wrong to generalize too sweepingly about Restoration Comedy. The plays of William Congreve, though included in this kind of comedy, came much later than those of Etherege. In *Love for Love* (1695) and *The Way of the World* (1700), we see comedy moving away from sparkling if brittle depiction of manners to the mode of sentimentalism which was to dominate the eighteenth century.

Congreve's dialogue has an impressive suppleness in its wit than other dramatists like Etherege's where dialogue often seems studied, over-consciously aphoristic. His characters too insist on keeping the masks on; they too believe in style, but Congreve manages to suggest the reality of human conditions at the end of *The Way of the World.* The play is a satire of manners and he uses the complicated relationships among the characters to point out the foibles of this callous and self seeking society.

The dramas of William Wycherley (1640-1716), especially *The Country Wife* (1675) and *The Plain Dealer* (1676), reach back to the works of the great masters, the first to Ben Jonson's *Volpone* and Moliere's *The School of the Wives* (1669) and later to *The Misanthrope*. This does not, however, mean that Wycherley stands outside, or apart from the general ethos of Restoration Comedy.

In *The Country Wife,* the Majory pinch wife shows that ultimately what Restoration Comedy dramatizes most confidently is the artifice and convention of the society it reflects. It was inevitable that the cynicism of

Restoration Comedy, especially in its earlier phase, should produce a reaction. Even from the time of Congreve, the beginnings of the movement from the Comedy of Manners to the Sentimental Comedy were under way.

Goldsmith's play, *She Stoops to Conquer* (1773) is his best attempt to write such a Sentimental Comedy as it makes skillful use of basic comic situations and in the character of Tony Lumpkin offers a pleasing reminder of the richness of Shakespearean clowns who are stupid and shrewd at the same time.

R.B. Sheridan (1751-1816) who was in favour of Comedy of Manners, wished to banish Sentimental Comedy from the stage. His comedy *The Rivals* has all the sparkle of Restoration Comedy, though the characters are more interested in marriage than in sexual intrigues. His *School for Scandal* is a fine exposure of the scandalmongers like Benjamin Backbile, Lady Sneerwell and is highly entertaining but also makes its point.

The elegance and verbal felicity of Sheridan's writing predicts, over the comic waste land of the next century, the superbly brilliant repartee of Oscar Wilde. His *The Importance of Being Earnest* revels in its own improbability and absurdity, consistently farcical in tone, characterization and plot.

Before coming to Modern Drama, mention may be made of Melodrama and Well-Made play. Melodrama was the most popular form of drama in the nineteenth century. Melodrama observes strict moral justice: good and evil are embodied in stock characters, in predictable action, and often in an explicit moral. We can see its followers both in France and Germany.

Following on the heels of Melodrama's popularity, a new form-Well-Made play-made its debut in France. Its popularity can be attributed to Augustan Eugene Scribe. In his plays, we can see a careful exposition of the situation; careful preparation of future events, growing suspense, unexpected reversals and a logical resolution. The term Well-Made play was originally used as a compliment to describe the tightly knit plots for which Scribe became famous.

Henerik Ibsen may be regarded as the father of Modern Drama. He is seen as a social realist concerned with the special issues relevant to his day and age. His plays like *The Pillars of the Society* (1877), *A Doll's House* (1879) and *Ghosts* (1881), dealing with the small town corruption, women's rights, venereal disease, brought a revolutionary new kind of social reality on to the European stage.

From these kinds of topics was distilled what Shaw calls Quintessence of Ibsenism-an essay on Ibsen by George Bernad Shaw written in 1891. He is seen-as a sort of expert consultant doctor, standing by the bedside of the sick patient (society), making a series of diagnosis of specific diseases, and dolling out the appropriate prescriptions.

He also employed an intensely dramatic method. He switched to prose after writing many plays in verse because he found it an appropriate medium for his vision of exploring ordinary existence. He is not only interested in verisimilitude, mere surface realism, reproduction of life like, probable speech, behavior and environment but delves deep beneath it and unfolds an intense psychological drama.

In *Hedda Gabler,* Hedda is married into a claustrophobic family completely hostile to her conception of herself as a free, proud and aristocratic spirit. The realistic surface details enable us to penetrate that surface to the hidden truth beneath. The real inner center of Ibsen's drama is its portrayal of the fundamental clash between man and society. This prevents his plays from seeming dated and gives some of them what many feel a tragic intensity.

Ibsen believed in individualism, that it was man's nature to strive to achieve the fullest realization of his selfhood and his belief in this freedom is built into all his great protagonists. He does not advocate superficial changes in social structure but rather with fundamental opposition between man's individualistic aspirations and his bondage to societal forces. Ibsen makes us see this battle with the self that an individual discovers with himself rather than individual confronts unyielding society in a somewhat melodramatic way.

Both Shaw and Brecht, like Ibsen, derive their dramatic ideas and form from a consideration of man's relationship with society. Shaw was a socialist and Brecht a Marxist. But their dramas differ in spirit and texture from that of Ibsen, whom Shaw greatly admired. As Shaw presented Ibsen in the Quintessence of Ibsenism, he is seen as a social reformer whose chief contribution is his exposure of outmoded or repressive codes and attitudes—social, political, moral and sexual. This is very much an Ibsen in Shaw's image. Shaw in his work attacked the current morality and ideology of the late Victorian Britain.

In his plays like *Arms and The Man, Man and Superman* and *Major Barbara,* he satirizes the blind orthodoxies of current idealizations of military glory and romantic love, the common cult of respectability, and dramatizes the falsity of the notion that poverty is in some way connected with moral worth. Shaw shows his slum dwellers and unemployed working class as cynical, hypocritical, aggressive and obsequious.

In short, he sees poverty as demoralizing. Shaw seems to resemble Plato in general outlook because both were concerned with ethical reform and insisted that art should be socially useful. He was interested in drama of ideas. He himself said in the 1902 Preface to *Mrs. Warren's Profession* that —the drama of pure feeling is no longer in the hands of the playwright; it has been conquered by the musician and there is, flatly, no future now, for any drama except the drama of thought.

His plays are only dramatized debates where characters are only mouthpieces for his ideas. No, they are driven emotionally, spiritually as well as intellectually by their ideas which constitute any given character's outlook on or approach to life and hence are more than philosophical debates. He also proposed his theory of creative evolution, which he called life force. This is actually optimistic and melioristic view that the universe is purposeful, that there is working in everyman, especially the philosopher, what in *Man and Superman* is called—life's incessant aspiration to higher organization, wider, deeper, in tenser self-consciousness, and clear self-understanding.

Major Barbara represents a significant step forward for a drama with a political or social message. The true resolution of Shaw's plays, as with many Brecht's play's, belongs not inside the work itself, but outside it, in society. The audience is left to think out the problems which Shaw has raised. The audience has to imagine a world in which power would be in moral hands and direction towards worthy ends. So Shaw's plays are engaged directly with major social issues as Brecht said of him.

Brecht became a Marxist in early 1930's and this affected the thrust and direction of his art and underpins his mature dramas like *Mother Courage and Her Children, The Life of Galileo, The Good Woman of Szechwan* and *The Caucasian Chalk Circle,* all written in exile. His plays embody a radical extension of Shaw's socialist ideas, but in no sense are regarded as simplistic propaganda pieces. His theoretical optimism is heavily qualified by his sense of cowardice, cruelty and destructiveness of human nature. He avoids the facile optimism by concentrating on why the world should be changed, rather than how it will be after the change.

He uses Marxism as a weapon for criticizing society as it is, and is not interested in creating utopian portraits of an ideal world, based purely on dogma. He rejected the naturalist drama which he calls Aristotelian or dramatic or Ibsenite' drama and this rejection lead to his own influential theory of drama.

He believed that it creates a total illusion of reality and objects to its verisimilitude, that is, its presentation of events, people and settings on the stage in such a way as to persuade the audience to suspend disbelief and to take the illusion for reality. Raymond Williams says,-What Brecht seized on was the exclusion, by particular conventions of verisimilitude, of all direct commentary, alternative consciousness, and alternative points of view.

In place of Aristotelian theatre, he created his own Epic Theatre which might be better termed as open theatre, because most of the techniques which he invents for plays like *Mother Courage and Her Children* are aimed at changing the relationship between play and its audience in the direction of openness. His techniques invite the audience to consider critically possible alternatives courses of action to those adopted by the dramatic characters, and insist that theatre is only a theatre and that plays are not life but they may help us to understand it.

Brecht rejects plot in favour of narrative. Each scene can be taken by itself; often long periods of time separate them. In it, we see action as a continuing process. The outcome of the action is open', not predetermined: what happens depends on human decision, not on some abstract concept like fate or inevitability. Mother Courage curses war when Kattrin is slashed across the eye and forehead.

In scene VII, she is happy because her business works well. Attention is switched away from Courage's emotional core, on to the incidents which she responds to. Brecht creates an antidote to theatrical illusion. Audience is aware that he is in the theatre and barrier between audience and stage is lowered. The whole point of the Epic Theater is to allow for, invite, stimulate critical attitude to what is presented and the breadth of perspective which Brecht brings to bear enables the audience to see the validity of the anti-heroic stance, but also its limitations in the particular context.

Modern Drama would be incomplete without the mention of Samuel Beckett. His plays opened up new possibilities for the stage in their exploration of the nature and limitations of theatre and their exploration of the limitations of language. In order to push the limits of drama, he exposed away virtually all of the traditional elements of theatre by employing spare settings, few actors and nothing in the way of conventional action. Action in his plays has progressed to inaction.

Though Brecht wishes the audience to approach critically from critical reaction to his plays, Beckett breaks the boundaries between stage and audience because he has the feelings that what is called real life is as much an illusion as anything on the stage. Beckett is referred as an Absurd dramatist, a term popularized by Martin Esslin (a dramatist, Professor of drama, best known for his term-The Theatre of Absurd|| for his work of the same name).

In his plays, there are feelings that are widely spread in the present times. The feeling that God is dead is significant and this deprives man of the sense of the transcendental purpose of life whose only object seems to be death. Beckett's plays don't tell a story but only represent a situation or condition and it throws man on his little resources to attempt to give significance left by the disappearance of the God.

The two tramps in *Waiting for Godot* employ various strategies to fill the void left and give them the impression that they exist. Estragon says, —We always find something to give the impression that we exist. Beckett like Albert Camus is relevant in exposing the symptoms of the apparent existence. However, they observe that the ultimate destiny of man is tragic.

Man is destined to suffering and despair on this planet. When we look at Beckett's work, it reveals that he employs the poetics of fragmentation and his characters live between the world of becoming and being, hell and heaven, mind and heart, faith and despair. His characters are not only physically deformed but also mentally disintegrated.

They are aware that they suffer without any fault of theirs. They see their life as a journey from nowhere to nowhere. Beckett and his characters remain lost in the fragments or thought, language, despair and useless repetition of broken, meaningless distorted and reshaped sentences and words.

In his texts, we see pauses, silences and dotted lines and his genius lies in exposing the insufficiency and incomprehensibility of language in so far as the perception and communication of reality is concerned. He subverts the very foundation of language, as there is no traditional plot development or lengthwise character portrayal in his works.

In *Waiting for Godot*, nothing happens twice as no one comes nor goes and everything becomes awful. His ultimate insight is full of doubt, despair and dread because his mind convinces him that nothing exists outside mind. His search is merely reason oriented. Having negated all supra-rational reality in order to discover personality and sentimentality which is beyond human reason, he loses himself in the abyss of Absurd and irrationality.

His people are God obsessed and struggle very hard to experience him. They ask why they are what they are and why are they conscious and their search starts from void, the nothing that lies behind reality. His characters search their true seat to escape suffering but they fail because the very search becomes obstacle.

Harold Pinter is also one of the most powerful talents to emerge in the Britain in the twentieth century. His best-known plays include *The Birthday Party* (1957), *The Homecoming* (1964) and *Betrayal* (1978). His talent remained disguised and his work misunderstood because his early plays coincided with the neo-realistic movement on the stage and was sometimes referred to as kitchen sink art.

There was the seedy realism of his settings, references to London and its environs and above all, there was his wonderful accuracy of dialogue, his talent for creating the speech patterns of working class or working middle class English people.

Drama originated as a form of low entertainment, passed through different stages and influenced writers from different corners of the world. It travelled from Greek theatrical performances to England, where it found writers like Christopher Marlowe, William Shakespeare and Ben Jonson and also reached the territories of Rome and France.

In the meantime, it experienced various changes in technical aspects as well as in thematic concerns. It reached to various countries like Ireland, Africa, America and India and developed into the genre of world acclaim with philosophical, political and socio-cultural orientations.

India has a long history of drama from ancient times. Its journey begins from Sanskrit plays. Indian tradition preserved in *Natyashastra* the oldest of the texts of the theory of drama, claims for the drama a divine origin, and a close connection with sacred Vedas themselves. Thus the origin of Indian drama is found in the Vedic period.

The most celebrated dramatists of the ancient era are Ashwagosh, Bhasa, Shudraka, Kalidasa, Harsha, Bhavbhuti, Vishakhadatta. Tragedies like *Urubhanga*, romances like *Abhijnana-sakuntalam* and historical plays like *Mudrarakshas* are the well known works of the Vedic period. The literature in Sanskrit is classified into two categories-*Drishya* (that can be seen) and the *Sravya* (that can be heard).

Drama falls in the catageory of *Drishya.* Drama in Sanskrit literature is covered under the broad umbrella of "rupaka" which means depiction of life in its various aspects represented in forms by actors, who assume various roles.

The Indian English Drama is supposed to have begun in the 18th century when the British Empire strengthened its power in India. It is taken to have started with the publication of Krishna Mohan Banerjee's *The Persecuted* in 1813. It is a social play which presents the conflict between the East and the West.

The real journey of Indian English drama begins with Madhusudan Dutt's *Is This Called Civilization* which was published in 1871. He also translated his play *Ratnavali* (1859) and *Sermista* (1859) originally written in *Bangla* into English. Rankinoo Dutt wrote his *Manipura Tragedy* in 1893. Indian English drama exhibited its genius after a long time in the 20th century.

The Pre Independence era witnessed the emergence of many significant playwrights. They were Rabindranath Tagore, Aurobindo Ghosh, T.P. Kailasam, A.S.P. Ayyar, Harindranath Chattopadhyaya, Bharati Sarabhai who made a tremendous contribution to the evolution and development of Indian English drama. R.N. Tagore and Sir Aurobindo Ghosh, the two great sage poets, are the first Indian dramatists of repute including Harindranath Chattopadhyaya, they are known as the big three who made an abiding contribution to the Indian English drama.

R.N. Tagore was awarded the Nobel Prize for literature and was considered as the epitome of Indian spiritual heritage. He wrote his plays primarily in *Bangla* but almost all his plays were translated into English. Some of them were translated by Tagore himself while the others, by Indian and English translators.

His best known plays *Chitra, Sacrifice, The Post Office, Muktadhara, The Cycle of Spring, The King of the Dark Chambers* are the examples of Indian philosophy. Tagore was the first among those who used symbolism and allegorical significance as a prime technique in their plays. He combined the Indian and the Western literary traditions to present a synthesis between the East and the West.

Sri Aurobindo (1872-1950) was also a major Indian English playwright. During 1891-1916, he wrote five complete and six incomplete verse plays. One of the most interesting features of his plays is the variety of periods (ranging from ancient Greece to medieval India) and places (diverse lands including Iraq, Syria, India, Spain, Britain and Norway). The two major themes of his plays are the idea of human evolution and love. All his plays are steeped in poetry and romance. The famous plays are *Perseus the Deliverer, The Viziers of Bassora, Prince of Edur, Eric, Vavadutta* and *Savitri.*

Sri Aurobindo employs ancient legends to highlight the contemporary urge for freedom and bondage and heighten the elements of heroism, adventure and mystery in the actions of his imaginary characters and as such, all his plays are imbued with a strong romantic impulse which appears to be the driving force behind all his plays.

In spite of his vast learning, he seems to have overlooked the rich tradition of Indian drama especially dramatic techniques. In order to express his romantic impulse, he has focused largely on the models of Elizabethan Drama. His plays are either in verse or a mixture of prose and verse. At times, he shows his ability in composing realistic dialogues in colloquial English. Regarding themes, he does not confine himself to one particular country and locales.

Last of the great Indian playwright trio, Harindranath Chattopadhyaya added a new dimension to Indian English drama. He was deeply influenced by the Progressive Writers" Movement. Like Mulk Raj Anand, he sympathizes with the underdogs. He has been more eminent as a poet than a playwright. His social plays highlight social protest and ideas of revolution.

His plays fall under four groups: Devotional, Social, Historical and Miscellaneous ones. *Five Plays* (1937) is a collection of his social plays-*The Windows, The Parrots, The Santry Lantern, The Coffin* and *The Evening Lamps.* These plays are marked by realism and have a didactic purpose.

In his social plays, Chattopadhyaya aims at presenting social evils and problems through symbols. In order to make presentation more effective, he presents many of his characters and situations in sharp contrast to one another. In his plays, he concentrates on a single topic which is an important feature of a short play. So far as models and techniques are concerned,

Chattopadhyaya seems to have been less influenced by Western drama in regard to the depiction of the lives of the saints.

Chattopadhyaya's social themes show his commitment to the Progressive Writers" Movement of the time, and symbolically present social problems like the problems of labour class, the evils of British rule. He sometimes indirectly suggests solutions to such problems.

A.S.P. Ayyar (1899-1963) is the next great dramatist in Indian English drama. He is primarily a social reformer who believes in exposing the ills of the contemporary Indian society. His first play is *In the Clutches of the Devil* and the last one is *The Trial of Science for the Murder of Humanity.* In Ayyar"s plays plot and characters are secondary as the message is given great importance.

He writes drama with ethical and social purpose by raising questions against widowhood, religious orthodoxy, superstition and hypocrisy. Ayyar handles the prose medium effectively and he is seen to be a vigorous critic of contemporary life.

A.S.P. Ayyar published a collection of three playlets, viz, *Sita's Choice, Brahma's Way* and *The Slave of Ideas* in 1935. His plays mostly dealt with discussions about the conflicting opinions on social customs. *Sita's Choice* is a play in five acts based on the theme of widow-marriage. *Brahma's Way* cannot be called a play as it is merely an interesting discussion on religious matters such as the existence of God, the caste-system in its right spirit, the unity among the three schools of Indian philosophy, vegetarianism, widow-marriage, balance between the material and spiritual aspects of life etc. the play is almost without a plot and the characters have their set attitude.

D. M. Borgaonkar"s three-act problem-play *Image-Breakers* (1938) is the presentation of the growing discontent of the youth in India and their revolt against the conventional marriage system which cares only for caste, horoscope, wishes of the elders, dowry and totally discarding emotions and feelings of human beings.

The conflict between love and social barriers is the theme of S. Fyzee-Rahamin"s *Daughter of Ind* (1940) which has three acts with a prologue and an epilogue and it deals with the deep love of low-caste girl for an idealistic English-man. Balwant Gargi"s *The Vulture* and other play (1941) is a collection of four playlets: *The Vulture*, *Mung-Wa*, *The Fugitive* and *The Matriarch*. He too seems to be interested in the social problems. Harindranath Chattopadhyaya remarks, Balwant Gargi has dealt with themes which are engaging the attention of people everywhere.

T.P. Kailasam (1885-1946) is another worth considering dramatist on the Indian literary scene. He wrote both in English and Kannada. His dramatic genius is fully expressed in his English plays such as *The Burden* (1933), *Fulfillment* (1933), *The Purpose* (1944), *Karna* (1946), *Keechaka* (1949). However, he was regarded as the father of modern Kannada drama.

In regard to models and techniques, Kailasam shows his inclination towards the Elizabethan drama. In spite of having reverence for the rich past of Indian dramatic tradition, he too seems to ignore it. He uses prose in dialogue, sometimes blank verse and sometimes a mixture of both.

Bharati Sarabhai (b.1912) is the maiden woman playwright who gave the Gandhian touch to Indian drama in English. Her two plays *The Well of the People* (1943) and *Two Women* (1952) are inspired by Gandhian philosophy.

The play *The Well of the People* is a poetic pageant than a play. It is highly symbolical.

This play is about an old woman who builds a well for the untouchables of her village which clearly shows the influence of Gandhi. Sarabhai, though a high caste woman, became an ardent follower of Gandhiji and worked in his Sabarmati Ashram. She had no practical experience of writing for theatre.

Moved by a story published in *Harijan*, Bharati Sarabhai wrote *The Well of the People*. The concept that God is within, is conveyed through this play. The same idea is expressed in *Two Women* in another way. The character Kanakaraya comes into conflict with his wife Anuradha who has decided to go to Himalayas in her quest for spiritual peace. At last, Kanakaraya gives up his rigid stand but his sudden death bring a new realization to his wife.

Sarabhai attempts to combine the ancient religion of India and the new culture. The old woman in *The Well of the People* acts as her mouthpiece in this regard. Sarabhai extends her theme of the practical realization of God in her play *Two Women* in a different way. The two women who represent the two faces of modern Indian womanhood are Anuradha, the wife of Kanakaraya and Urvashi, the widowed girl who becomes a devotional singer.

The two women seem to be complementary, and true to *Vedantic* thought, they prove that God can be found everywhere. Sarabhai treats her themes in relation to the Indian tradition. The blend of material and the spiritual is focused. She takes her characters from the traditional world and leads them to the ultimate reality of the omnipresence of God.

The Pre Independence phase presents the large number of writers who preferred to write short plays in comparison to the full length plays. So far as the themes are concerned, social issues were prominent in the plays of this period. The plays dealing with legendary and historical themes occupied the place next to the social plays.

Some of the writers drew their themes from ancient myth and legends and interpret them in terms of a contemporary social problem as in *Perseus the Delieverer* by Sri Aurobindo. Bharati Sarabhai and Krishnaswami also tried their hands in this direction. Playwrights like Kailasam and Ramaswami Sastri showed their interest either in highlighting the greatness of epic heroes and heroines or in giving importance to the neglected characters.

Regarding social themes, many playwrights like Chattopadhyaya, Ayyar and Narayanan focus on the burning problems of contemporary society whereas V.V.S. Aiyangar and others made a farcical and melodramatic presentation of some problems. History and current politics drew the attention of only a few like A.S.P. Ayyar, Annayya and Mrinalini Sarabhai.

As regards models and techniques, most of the playwrights opted for the Elizabethan model. Sri Aurobindo adopted the Elizabethan models. Kailasam drew inspiration from Shakespeare for plot construction. Many playwrights did not adhere to the classical Sanskrit Drama and ancient techniques. Many follow neither the Western nor the Indian tradition and show little sense of dramatic strategy as their main interest appears to lie in composing dialogue for discussion of topics of their choice.

Further, in case of few playwrights, the acts which their works are supposed to consist of are nothing but scenes and this shows a lack of understanding of the structure of a play. Language also came out as a big problem to almost all the playwrights of the phase. Though they tried to overcome the problem in their own way but could not succeed. Sri Aurobindo's long speeches created obstruction in the action of his plays.

While Kailasam tried to enhance the beauty of his language with his excessive rhetoric and archaism. Chattopadhyaya, Ayyar and others showed their command on the style of writing but it gave way to the artificiality of their dialogue on the stage. On the whole, most of the playwrights did not write stage worthy plays. Their plays meant to be read only.

Indian English Drama showed little progress in the Post-independence period. Though the efforts were made but it could not gain much. The Five Year Plans after the Independence encouraged performing arts as an effective medium for public enlightenment and healthy entertainment. Institutions like National School of Drama was established in Delhi, Institutions for training in dramatic art were founded in many cities; Departments of Drama were opened in many universities.

The National Drama Festival was started in Delhi by the Sangeet Natak Akademi. But all those developments promoted the growth of drama in regional languages. Though the Theatre Group in Bombay and some other agencies did successfully stage Indian English drama yet these performances could not give much popularity to Indian English drama. By and large, plays written in regional languages dominated the Indian theatre.

As a result of these advancements, many writers started writing plays meant for the stage. In this group, there are several writers. Nissim Ezekeil, Girish karnad, Pritish Nandi, Pratap Sharma and Murli Das Melwani are some of the writers of this group who contributed in the development of Indian theatre.

Nissim Ezekiel who has made a distinctive contribution to poetry wrote six plays on the themes-hollowness of urban middle class, futility of social mores and the institution of marriage. The *Three Plays* (1969) consists of *Nalini*, a comedy in three acts, *Marriage Poems*, a one act tragic-comedy and

The Sleepwalkers an Indo-American farce. *Song of Deprivation* is a one act comic morality play dealing with the theme of suppression and repression.

After a period of twenty years, he wrote the play *Don't Call it Suicide*-a socio psychological analysis of suicide. *Nalini* is about the hollow life of two advertising executives, Bharat and Raj. In this, the playwright projects two pictures: the hollow world of the young executives and the contrast between the two Nalini-the one of the dream and the other of reality.

In all three plays, Ezekiel remains content by projecting the cross-section of contemporary society. He does not give as much importance to the development of a plot as to the composing brilliant conversations. Thus, in spite of the stage-directions and sound effects suggested by author, these plays could not meet the full demands of the stage.

Unlike Ezekiel"s picture of urban society, Arati Nagarwalla"s three-act play *The Bait* (1969) deals with the loyalty of a villager and his love for justice. Knowing his wife is killed by a lion in a forest, Panna, the hero of the play, takes the oath to avenge her death. He kills the animal and is arrested on the charge of attempted homicide.

Girish Karnad is a living legend in the contemporary Indian English drama. He is a playwright, actor, critic and a film star. He has received recognition nationally as well as internationally. His five plays *Tuglaq, Hayavadana, Nagamandala, Tale-Danda* and *The Fire and the Rain* have been translated into English, the first two by Karnad himself.

His plays are steeped in Indian culture as the themes are taken from myths, legends, folk tales and history. He combines classical, folk and the Western dramatic techniques in his plays. He has made a great contribution to Indian English drama.

Vijay Tendulakar (1928-2008) can be considered as the precursor of modern Indian English drama. His plays focus on the conflicts between the individual and the society. The angry and frustrated protagonists of his plays are actually the victims of harsh circumstances in life. Since he exposes the ugly side of the society, therefore, his plays are considered as controversial ones.

His plays are *Silence: The Court is in Session, Kamala, The Vultures, Sakharam Binder.* The major themes of his plays are male domination, violence, exploitation of women and rejection of social norms. He explores human mind and its complexities in all its depth and variety. He does not present human relation in relation to love and emotions but in sensuality and violence.

2. GIRISH KARNAD

Girish Raghunathan Karnad was born in Matheran, Maharastra to Rao Saheb Dr. Karnad and Krishna Bai Mankeekara on 19th May 1938. He is contemporary writer, playwright, screenwriter, actor and movie director in Kannada language. His initial schooling was in Marathi. In Sirsi, Karnataka, he was exposed to travelling theatre groups, Natak Madalis as his parents were deeply interested in plays.

Girish Karnad went to England to join the Oxford University with a scholarship. He secured on merit. He left for England from Mumbai. His performance in Oxford was good and he even thought of settling down in UK. However, the appreciation and accolades for his first play *Yayati*. After returning to India, he worked in Oxford University Press, Madras for seven years. He married Saraswathi at the age of forty two.

During the year 1987-88, he was at the University of Chicago as Visiting Professor. He served as the Director of the Film and Television Institute of India and Chairman of the Sangeet Natak Akademi, the National Academy of the performing Arts and director of the Nehru Centre and as Minister of Culture, in the Indian High Commission, London.

Karnad has received Sangeeta Nataka Akademi award in 1972, Padma Shri in 1974, Padma Bhushan in 1992, Kannada Sahitya Academy in 1992, Sahitya Academy award in 1994, Jnanapith Award in 1998, Kalidas Samman in and Rajyotsava Award in 1998. He also received honouary doctorate from University of Southern California, Los Angeles in 2011 and D.Litt from Karnataka University in 1994.

He has published an autobiography in 2011, Girish Karnad has written fourteen plays with English translations by him.

Indian English Drama has registered a remarkable growth and maturity through the English translation of Hindi, Marathi and the Bengali plays in the 1980s and the 1990s. A study of Karnad's works amply reveals that he has added a new dimension to Indian drama substantially. Taking an all-round view of things it may be said that Indian English drama has achieved a considerable measure of success.

Karnad's plays present a psychological interpretation of human history-not neither rational nor material, but the basic conflict of man, his littleness and limit ness, follies and faults of his life and the continuous struggle he is involved in. They not only represent the modern age but also relate at length the existing class conflicts, spiritual degradation, utter helplessness and self-agony, while dramatizing the inevitable process of life and death and an ultimate goal which dissolves all mundane desire into spiritual bliss and harmony.

Karnad's dramas are larger than life in their dimensions. We can read, explain and interpret them from various angles and different levels. They stand out as the culmination of Karnad's dramatic genius. They are steeped in mystery, myth of the creation of our society. Though rooted in antiquity the themes have universal dimension of men's predicament. They are not time-bound though they refer to different periods of history. They are ageless.

Even the modern reader finds so much of relevance of his contemporary world, his life and problem in them. They contain infinite variety and richness. Their appeal is-all embracing-emotional, intellectual and spiritual. They are the works of sublimity and magnitude. It is really creditable how Girish Karnad could present the subtle shades of emotional and revealed them in real motives that lie buried in the deep recesses of his characters minds. He also presented their spiritual and human predicament and, above all, a complex native cultural complexion in an alien language.

Karnad's dramatic world is most strange. Peeling the multiple layers of fantasy his protagonists seek to confront the mystery of life beyond the horizon. His plays represent a unique depiction of the dual between the intern al and the external, the intuitive and rationalistic tradition and modernity.

He catches the bewilderment of the individual psyches, confronted with the overbearing socio-cultural atmosphere and the ever-present modern promise of self-fulfilment. In the face of this conflict-crisis his Yayati, Tughlaq, Padmini, Rani, Bijjala and others are viewed from different angles of philosophical analysis.

Although, *Yayati* was a great king, he was also a human being. Like many rulers he was tempted at times to believe that he himself was above the law. When that happens the results are bound to be disasterous. One of the most flagrant examples was when he fell in love with Sharmishtha driven by the desire to have her as his wife. *Yayati* reminds us of a Biblical hero David who was a great leader. He fell in love with Bathsheba, the wife of Uriah, one of his leading generals.

Driven by the desire to have Bathsheba as his wife, David sent Uriah to certain death in battle. When he came to his senses however, David realized the terrible sin that he had committed. In the depth of remorse, he wrote the beautiful 'Fifty-first Psalm' which has been called one of the finest expressions of repentance in the Bible.

Yayati, too becomes penitent after Chitralekha's suicide. Karnad has reinterpreted the ancient myth in the light of the contemporary context.

Karnad's *Yayati,* (1961) initially written in Kannada, conveys the message of performance of duty and acceptance of responsibility. In this play, Karnad presents the age-old story of the mythological King Yayati who was the tenth in the line of the Brahma's family. Once a conflict arises between Devayani, the daughter of Shukracharya, the guru of the assuras, and Sharmistha the daughter of Vrishparva, the King of the assuras, and the latter pushed Devayani into a well and escaped.

Fortunately, King Yayati who came there saved her. Since then, Devayani started loving Yayati and Sharmistha was punished with serving Devayani forever along with her maidservants. With the consent of Shukracharya the marriage between Devayani and King Yayati was solemnized and Sharmistha as a result of her punishment was sent to King Yayati's kingdom along with his bride Devayani.

Sharmistha develops secret relationship with Yayati and when Devayani comes to know this she complains to her father, who in turn, curses Yayati to become old. Yayati is unable to bear this; he loses control over himself, becomes violent, adamant and refuses to accept the old age. When his son Puru informs that Yayati can be redeemed if some person accepts his old age, he becomes very happy.

When Puru informs that nobody is willing to take up his old age, he is unable to accept the reality as he is of the wrong notion that all his subjects would readily accept his old age. Karnad has portrayed the contours of the real world, i.e. when you laugh the world will laugh with you, but when you are in sorrow you will be alone, deserted even by your kith and kin. Yayati feels very much disheartened because old age had not come to him in its normal course but by a curse. So he feels that if somebody accepts it at present he would relieve him from his old age within five or six years.

In the play *Yayati,* Puru proves to be the best son as he gladly accepts the curse inflicted on his father and willingly exchanges his youth for the old age of his father. Though *Yayati* succeeds in transforming his old age and his sins to Puru, he acts in the most irresponsible way by usurping the happiness of his son and daughter-in-law. Rajinder Paul has commented that "the protagonist in Yayati asks for eternal youth which his son sacrifices at the altar of paternity, a very Indian theme of a self-denying son indulging the whim of his unreasonable father." (41)

In the process he feels disillusioned and looses faith. Though his sub-conscious mind tells him that it is not fair on his part, he justifies that it is only for his people he is doing like this. In actuality King Yayati exchanges his old age with the youth of his youngest son for the satisfaction of his own youthful urges. In the end Puru's wife Chitralekha commits suicide. Through this action the dramatist makes Yayati to accept his responsibility for the sin he had committed.

Yayati asks Puru to take back his youth and be a good king as he felt that there could be no better lesson than Chitralekha's death. He also asks Sharmistha to accompany him to the forest, as he has to wash his sins by doing penance in the forest. He finally says that he has spent his youth in the city but will spend his old age in the forest. When Chitralekha dies, her husband Puru is astonished, but he does not shed even a drop of tear. Only when he regains his youth he repents for the disastrous blunder he had committed.

It is pathetic that King Yayati and his son Puru realize their evil deeds only at the cost of a life, Chitralekha. The dramatist portrays the selfless nature and the helpless plight of the Indian women who, by willingly sacrificing their lives, make the members of their family to realize their nobility. Thus Indian women serve as a contrast to Indian men.

The dramatist, through the portrayal of the character of Yayati, focuses on the theme of attachment to life and its pleasures. Yayati realizes the horrors of his selfish action of exchange of youth in the later period, only after the suicide of his daughter-in-law and he readily owns the responsibility for the havoc that befell the family and returns the youth of his son Puru and retires to the forest as a hermit.

Through the life of Yayati, the dramatist brings out the fact that selfish paternal authority and blind filial loyalty could bring ruin to a family when it is misappropriated. Almost every character except Sharmistha is irresponsible. Yayati who is cursed for his adultery transfers the burden most irresponsibly to his son.

Puru, his son, who is married to Chitralekha and owes a dharmic responsibility to ensure her happiness, equally irresponsibly vitiates her marital bliss by exchanging his youth with his father for the sake of preserving the latter's happiness. He is caught between the devil and the deep sea-filial loyalty and conjugal felicity, and whichever he chose; he would still be caught in the web of irresponsibility.

Devayani acts impetuously, brings a curse upon her husband King Yayati, and runs away irresponsibly when he is visited by the ugly consequences of the curse. Chitralekha, unable to bear the consequences of her husband Puru's exchange of youth with his father, commits suicide instead of fighting to restore her rights.

Karnad's another play *Tughlaq* is also regarded as a contemporary play about a contemporary situation. It is called a minor classic of dramatic literature. Tughlaq's reign like king Soloman's began in glory but ended in near failure. Soloman failed for the heavy taxes which he had to impose upon the tribes in order to raise money for the magnificent temple which his father: David, had long dreamed to build in Jerusalem. This made him unpopular.

Tughlaq's changing of capital and currency became his hallmarks and which caused him considerable trouble. He miserably failed even to weld his people into a real notion, a powerful country and a united people. His dream was shattered. Even before his death one could see the shadow of coming events that would wreck the good that his ancestors had done. Man turns to God for help in times of troubles, discouragement and sorrow.

In *Tughlaq*, the stepmother plays the role of a composite mother preceptor figure. She is like a delicate fragile thread; she apparently keeps the totally estranged Muhammad humanly related. Despite his claim that he has never extended comparable love to anyone else, her affection for Muhammad remains genuine throughout. Her anxiety over his health and concern for his well-being speak volumes for her affection. She repeatedly counsels him to exercise restraint over his excessive desire for power and indulgence in violence. She pleads with Muhammad and says, "It's only seven years ago that you came to the throne. How glorious you were then, how idealistic, how full of hopes. Look at your kingdom now. It's become a kitchen of death." (10.204)

On the other hand, Najib tries to abet his contrary tendencies. Najib's politicking proves more effective than the stepmother's affection. Unable to tolerate this, she seeks the assistance of Barani, who is a symbol of wisdom imbibed through history. As he too proves helpless she has Najib assassinated. But as Nayak comments that "the monster in Muhammad cannot be eliminated by him or by others, it remains intact and is to be suffered, inevitably like fate" (2).

Tughlaq has turned out to be a monster to be accepted as fate: what cannot be changed must be tolerated, if not eliminated. But Tughlaq becomes furious, calls her as an adulteress and orders "I want her stoned to death publicly tomorrow morning" (10.205). Thus Tughlaq appears to be a Machiavellian ruler perpetuating his view and subduing women in all aspects. Karnad vividly portrays that most Indian women are not given the privilege to act on their own or reveal their anxieties or their feelings and if they do, they are to face drastic consequences.

Nagamandala makes a high achievement in the evolution of the playwright. By developing an Indian myth, the play creates a mysterious and powerful experience through the dual representation of the cobra and Appanna. They are inseparably connected in the tale, leading to a multi dimensional situation; Rani's transformation from the moment of her oath-taking heightens the suggestive quality of the play.

The personification of 'Story' and the 'Flames' and their action-oriented representation make the entire play very powerful and help to project a wide a range of human experience. The most fascinating in the play in the playwright's attempt to recreate the Kannada myth to portray the human predicament in a contemporary social situation. His wearing together of the Western and eastern concepts of the theatre language in interpreting the myth is evident in the development of a plot.

Naga-mandala of Girish Karnad presents the deplorable state of women in Indian Society. The playwright says in the prologue that man is a bundle of weakness, he is either not aware of them or he cannot get rid of them. The man fails to realize the significance of this prediction. He takes it literally and breaks into a laughter because he thinks that keeping awake one night is not a task, failing to realize that keeping awake will rather be a Herculian task for a man who dozes off the month, which can be the last night of his life also, he awakes up to the fact that he has to do something to avert his death.

He comes to dilapidated temple with an unidentifiable statue to pass his last night. But this temple is a favorite haunt of the flames that come from different houses so exchange notes on the present conditions of the society. The first flames come from the house of a miserly fellow who retires to bed early to save spending on lamp oil. The second tells in which the old mother has died neglected and third flame tells about the story of Rani whose predicament reflects the human need to live by fiction and half-truths.

The drama is enacted in a temple at night, in the presence of three naked flames, in front of a man cursed to die within a few hours. The new flame has a different story to tell. The old mistress has seen young women dressed in a Sari coming out of the room in, which her husband is sleeping. However this story also comes to the temple and desires that it should be heard by somebody who can pass it on to others. Flames cannot do it because they are non-living objects.

Act I presents the story of a young girl named Rani, who is the only child of her parents. She is also called Rani because she is the queen of long tresses. When her hair was tied up in a knot, it was as though a black cobra lay curled on the nape of her neck. Her father finds a match for her and gets her married to a young man who is rich and his parents are dead.

Rani's husband Appanna, proud and jealous, ill-treats her, coming home only during lunch and staying away with a concubine at night.

Kurudavva a best friend of Appannas mother is blind but her regard for her deceased friend outweighs her disability. She tells her son Kappanna that he keeps his wife locked up like a caged bird. Kurudavva is moved with pity. She asks Rani not to worry and sends Kappanna to bring the roots, which produce the magical quality of love in the heart of the man that eats them.

Kappanna gives the roots to Rani with the instruction. Grind it into a nice paste and feed it to your husband and watch the results. Once he smells you he won't go sniffing after that bitch. He will make you a wife instantly. According to Kappannas instruction she pours the paste into the curry. She pours this curry into the ant-hill. As she turned out of the ant-hill a cobra lifts its hood, hissing out of the ant-hill. Thus the cobra comes to love Rani.

The second Act presents the love story of Rani and the cobra. Appanna has brought a dog to keep the blind Kurudavva away from his wife. The dog is tied to the door. The cobra assumes the shape of Appanna to make love with Rani. He comes every night when Appanna is away. Rani gets confused on observing the nature of Appanna. Appanna becomes angry when he comes to know of the pregnancy of Rani.

When Rani is the position of proving her loyalty and chastity to the villager, she takes the, cobra in her hand. The cobra does not bite her, but slides up her shoulder and spreads it hood like an umbrella over her head. The crowd gets stunned while the elders declare her as a God, a divine being. Appanna asks her forgiveness and takes her fondly into his arms. Rani gives birth to a beautiful son, but Appanna knows the fact that he is not the father of the son.

The cobra, could not bear the separation, ties a tress of Ranis hair around his neck and strangles itself to death hiding in her hair. The dead cobra falls to the ground when Appanna combs her hair, Rani who now understands all about the cobra. Appanna accepts the wishes of Rani as he takes her as an incarnation of the goddess. The playwright's vision of the human and nonhuman worlds is revealed in this play.

In *Hayavadana*, Karnad exposes how women are exploited in the family.

Devadatta, a gentle scholar, falls in love with a beautiful and vivacious girl, Padmini. His friend Kapila, an ironsmith and figure of impressive physical stature acting as a matchmaker, realizes that Devadatta "Can't bear a bitter word or an evil thought", but Padmini is "fast as lightening-and sharp" (1.90).

Though Kapila realizes that Padmini needs a man of steel, he is unable to do anything and so he is committed to obtain her in marriage for his dear friend Devadatta. Ultimately the two families were brought together by the toll of marriage bells. A marriage in the Indian context is not something that takes place between two individuals but something that brings two families together. Bhagavata also describes the marriage of Devadatta and Padmini as two families coming together.

In *Hayavadana,* Karnad re-shapes an ancient Indian myth from the *veralapanchavimsati* to point to man's eternal quest for completeness, or self-realization. With its highly stylized action and mimicry, especially the scene at the temple of *Kali* and the sword fight between Devadatta and Kapila in the second act, Karnad invests the play with a significance, which brings out the emptiness of the incomplete human being.

In this play, the central figure is a woman, Padmini. Selfishness and sensuality find expression in her insatiable desire for both brain and brawn, which are symbolized by Devadatta and Kapila respectively. Married to Devadatta, Padmini craves for the muscle and body of Kapila. In the myth, and in the play as well, the craving is not explicit, it runs as an undercurrent in Padmini"s sub-conscious. She desires deeply for both the body and the intellect, though sub-consciously.

It is difficult to prophesy whether or not she would have behaved differently had there been a proper equation of physical strength and intellectualism in either Devadatta or Kapila. The happenings in the Kali temple, where she transposes the heads of Devadatta and Kapila, reveal her sub- conscious desire. Padmini's act, though unintentional, is indicative of the incomplete human beings silent cry for wholeness.

In other words, the re-enactment of the ancient myth in *Hayavadana* aims at the transformation of the fractured self into a composite whole. It has to be underlined that the transposition of heads, fails to solve Padmini"s problem of identity, which is at bottom a universal human problem of *Who am I ? What am I?* Padmini"s desires are not stated explicitly even after the transposition of heads.

The tension between moral right and wrong pervades her whole being. Immediately after finding out what she had done hastily and unintentionally, although she actually desires for Kapila"s body, she is in utter confusion.

The myth in the words of the Bhagavata offers the solution to Padmini's predicament: As the Heavenly *Kalpa vriksha* is supreme among trees, so is the head among human limbs. Therefore the man with Devadatta's head is indeed Devadatta and he is the rightful husband of Padmini. Thus the tale of the *Vetalapanchavimsati* acts as a metaphor for Karnad's narration of the psychological predicament of the modern man bound by social and moral norms and inhibitions.

Karnad does not take myths in their entirety. He takes them only in parts that are useful to him and the rest he supplements with his imagination. He combines the story of the transposed heads taken from Thomas Mann with the story of Hayavadana which is, in part, Karnad's own imagination and invention. While making use of an ancient myth, Karnad makes certain changes in the original myth. For example, he has changed the names of characters. He remarked that he had changed the names deliberately, for he wanted the names to be generic terms applying to all human beings, because the characters are all types.

When dealing with a theme like this, the moot question is how much of the folk tale structure should be retained and how much a contemporary perception should be induced into it. It is the age-old struggle between tradition and modernity, the combination of the unreal with the real, and the tussle between direct and literary portrayal with abstraction and stylization.

In *The Fire and the Rain*, Paravasu, the son of Raibhya, a great sage and the chief priest, is conducting a fire sacrifice for seven long years in the King's Palace in order to propitiate Lord Indra, the God of rains. Vishakha, his wife, was once loved by his cousin Yavakri, but when he left for the forest to seek enlightenment, the girl's father felt relieved, made use of the opportunity and married his daughter to Paravasu.

Though the girl "didn't want to" marry Paravasu, she acquiesces herself to the reality of her helpless situation and tells her father: "but that did'nt matter"(1.16). On the night of the wedding, her husband realizing that his newly wedded wife didn't wish to marry him, he says that he will make her "happy for a year. And he did. Exactly for one year (1.16).

He plunged her into a kind of bliss and made her feel heavenly. Then on the first day of the second year of their marriage, he puts an end to this and just leaves her accepting the invitation from the King to be the Chief Priest.

The site of the fire sacrifice is only a couple of hours away from his home. But in all those seven years he never came back. Vishakha feels very lonely and "become[s] dry like tender. Ready to burn into flames at a breath." (1.16)

The happy married life of this helpless woman lasts just for a year. She is a lonely figure, suffering the pangs of loveless marriage like most women in contemporary society. Ultimately she becomes a prey to Yavakri who seduces her just to take revenge against her father-in-law and her husband. Her father-in-law, the great sage Raibhya, also seduces her in order to gratify his lust.

Finally she is left without anybody even to share her agonies with. Her loneliness and humiliation reveal the pangs of such pathetic women in the modern world. In order to take revenge upon the Brahmanic society, she urges Yavakri to have sex with her. Through Vishakha, who is disgusted, suppressed, crushed, exploited and humiliated, the playwright shows the plight of most Indian women in a male dominating society.

She urges Yavakri to have sex with her. Through Vishakha, who is disgusted, suppressed, crushed, exploited and humiliated, the playwright shows the plight of most Indian women in a male dominating society. Whereas in the case of men those who are devoid of power and value are exploited and oppressed in the society, in the case of women, everyone irrespective of socio-economic status is exploited and oppressed- both at home and in the society.

Men are content with their power in the house, while women are content with their power on children and daughter-in-law. Taught to repress her own desires and trained to practice self-effacement, woman has come to articulate a male constructed definition, which she has internalized. Therefore when she speaks, it is patriarchy that speaks through her. She is not expected to go out and perform, but efficiently lurk around the threshold supporting the male endeavor.

Literature is replete with examples of women who meet with destruction because they try to cross the threshold. Those who happened to cross so, and acquire voice were scared of the wide, dark, animalistic devouring world outside and beat an undignified retreat to get inside the threshold.

But a large number of them remain committed, passive, servile and silent, bearing and rearing children, and gratifying the sexual needs of their husbands. Elements of discontent, unfulfilled desires and aspirations, unequal demands made by the other are stillborn and reborn. Men and women imbibe the exploitative and oppressive culture and perpetuate it. So, they fail to realize the reality. They blame one another, quarrel among themselves and make their life miserable. They do not try to eradicate the morbid culture that led to the pathetic state.

Tala-Danda too poses the problem of human identity in a world of human relationships Basavanna is Karnad's mouthpiece who leads a movement of reformation in protest against discrimination based on caste, class and gender. The play stresses the old adage that excess of everything is bad. As such, extremes of prejudice as well as piety result in the doom of all human endeavours for bringing out social change.

The political repercussions of activism of the reformers, the conflict of the various sects within and without affect the fate of common masses. The play opens before us some interesting and controversial sites of our ancient and medieval culture. Karnad's great awareness of the power of caste consciousness alienation and the politics of riots make this play a novel experiment of orthodox Hindu society.

In *Tale–Danda*, when King Bijjala's son Sovideva is raging against the Sharanas who have made a fool of him in the treasury episode, Rambhavati, the Queen, plainly tells her son, "Do as you wish. Just don't upset your father, that's all. He turns his bad temper on me and I can't take it any longer" (1.2.8). When Sovideva accuses her of being under the spell of the sharana's mystic–saint leader Basavanna, she says, "What am I to do? Do you think your father ever listens to me?" (1.2.8).

There is hardly a hint of equality in the husband–wife relationship. She might be the queen of the kingdom but the reality is that she is no better than any other servant of the palace as far as the King is concerned. She has to wail and cry and shed tears to persuade Bijjala to leave sharana alone. It is not that he does not love her. He is fond of her and cares for her. But the deep-rooted patriarchal attitude makes him feel superior and behave in a rude manner.

Sovideva's wife also remains in the same situation. Sovideva neglects his wife, sends her to her parents, and does not bother to bring her back. She does not interfere with her husband's matter, who wantonly revels in the arms of a prostitute, Indrani. But Sovideva's wife, the voiceless woman, acquires value when Sovideva is scared, confused and in dire need of help after beheading Madhuvarasa and Haralayya. When Manchanna says to Sovideva that the queen's "support may come in handy", Sovideva answers: "Yes. And see our Queen again! She is our Queen after all, frigid bitch though she is" (3.11.80). Women are valued not because she is a human being but only for her functional utility.

The most important event in the play is the marriage between a Brahmin's daughter and a cobbler's son. The girl's mother Lalitamba's reluctance to the marriage is not given due importance because it is her husband Madhuvarasa's decision which matters. Lalitamba points to the practical problems besetting the alliance of a Brahmin girl with a cobbler boy.

The glaring paradox of disjointed happenings and helplessness are the prevalent in public life in our country. Like Basavanna, a man's mystic quest is solitary-a truth that cannot be communicated in verbal terms, it can be felt. The totality of the world remains deceptive.

The *Dreams of Tipu Sultan* is a kannada play written in 1997 by Indian playwright Girish Karnad. The story follows the last days as well as the historic moments in the life of the Ruler of Mysore, Tipu Sultan, through the eyes of an Indian court historian and a British Oriental scholar.

The figure of Tipu Sultan has continued to dominate Indian and British imagination for over two centuries, as attested by the numerous scholarly works, ballads, plays and novels about his tempestuous life and tragic end. *The Dreams of Tipu Sultan* examines the inner life of the warrior, political visionary and dreamer.

The English fought four Anglo-Mysore wars against Tipu Sultan to defeat him and gain control over Mysore. Tipu Sultan did not agree to cede with the British demands like the Nizam and Marathas. The British started their operations against srirangapatna early in 1792 A.D. The English army marched against the fort and arrived in the sight of the fortress on the 16th February 1792 A.D.

On the same night, the operations started and the English pushed Tipu's force to the fort and captured the island except the fort. Helplessly Tipu proposed the peace treaty on 23rd of February 1792 A.D. As per the treaty, Tipu agreed to surrender half of his territory to the English and pay three crores thirty lakhs rupees as war indemnity.

Since he could not pay war indemnity in full, he accepted to send his second and third sons namely Abdul Kahliq and Maiz-Uddin aged 10 and 8 respectively as hostages till he would pay the due. He paid the balance amount and got them after two years at Devanahalli.

After the Third Mysore war, Tipu Sultan sent envoys to Persia, France and Afghanistan to seek help from them in fighting against the English. He contacted Napoleon Bonaparte also. Though he accepted to help Tipu against the English because of his failure against the English, he could not keep his word. Tipu then planned a holy war against the English along with Afghanistan. This failed because of the timely intervention of Wellesley.

Considering these strategies of Tipu Sultan, Wellesley wrote a letter to Tipu Sultan on 8th of November 1798 A.D complaining that Tipu was working against the Treaty of Srirangapatna. He suggested resolving the problems through discussion. Wellesley's suggestions were ignored by Tipu. The English declared a war against him. In 1799 A.D Srirangapatna was seized by the English after killing Tipu Sultan in what was to be the fourth and final Mysore war.

There are two views about Tipu Sultan: one view holds him as a dictator and Muslim fanatic; the other view sees him as tolerant of other religions, as a learned person with foresight and great military powers. Concentrating on the later view, Karnad intends to show Tipu not merely as a warrior Chieftain of the 18th century, but also as a visionary.

The play presents Tipu Sultan as a visionary who wishes for the dawn of a new era. His vision for the future is of an India free from clutches of colonization. He wants to thoroughly wipe out the English from the face of India. In his last dream, he fancies the British retreating from the battle field. He jumps in joy even as he dreams, he fancies the British retreating from the battle field. His visions include not only the removal of the English from the Indian soil, but also the establishment of a great empire like them. He aims to acquire military power by gaining economic power, which he believes is to be gained through trade is the way to prosperity.

Tipu Sultan's vision for his kingdom was deeply rooted in his ambition and desire of developing into a progressive, powerful force in India. It is the unwillingness in Tipu's contemporaries to accept his ideas of trade and vision to bring about a social change that paves the way for his fall. Tipu's initiative to globalize gives rose to many problems and conflicts which finally prove disastrous for him. Karnad has succeeded in portraying Tipu as an ardent reformer and a zealous visionary whose ardor and zeal fail to reconcile his dreams with his people's live.

Like an Indian writer in English he is in a peculiar position. He is deeply rooted in the native tradition but like a tree getting its life juice from roots; it has to breathe in the surrounding air. And air, in his plays, is full of modernity. He is fully aware of the predicament of man and has tried to bring about a happy and harmonious union of the tradition of the East and West of old and modern of myths and facts. He does it because he concluded that without any new stage of human development would fall as soon as it is erected.

The values of art science and ethics are all integrated into a fuller and clearer sense of essential formative forces at work within the man. He asserts that the madness in exploitation and war for material gains leads to a degeneration of the soul and corrupts it forever. It is this soul stirring quality that raises him to a place of prominence among the writers of English drama. The picture of men and women ruthlessly trampled under the heels of the stupid and callous tyranny of the privileged; few touch the springs of human pity.

Influenced by the western literary and philosophical obsession in Camus, Sartre, Malamud and other American writers Karnad finds it a fashionable craze to write about the modern crisis-crisis of identity, existential chaos almost in the same manner in which the seventeenth century English authors simulated to be melancholy: He knows that worldly affluence is not enough. The one world is dead and the other is powerless to be born.

The escape from the outer world to the inner world, keeps man engaged. Therefore, Karnad's major characters find themselves in a situation from which they find it difficult to get disentangled. Thus, in the depiction of existentialism in the postmodern world in the wake of colonial hangover, economic depression, psychological split-up as well as existential angst and freedom of choice in his plays Karnad is unparalleled.

3. MAHESH DATTANI

Mahesh Dattani is the most powerful and potent dramatic voice in the present Indian English dramatic world. He has enriched and embellished the tradition of Indian Drama with his experiments and innovations. With the arrival of Mahesh Dattani on the literary scene, the scenario begins to change. His plays are written in English. He has authored a good number of dramas diverse in themes, techniques and devices.

The plays of Mahesh Dattani are characterized by some theatrical and thematic innovations. He has not only intellectual power and prowess to produce a play in text but also has an ability to get it staged successfully. The plays of Mahesh Dattani are characterized by some theatrical and thematic innovations. His work is a confluence of art and craft.

He has an unconventional approach to theatre. He looks at the theatre as the medium to manifest the cause of the unprivileged segments of our society. His plays externalize the problems and pent up feeling of the subalterns in a very authentic and realistic manner. In his plays, Dattani visits untraversed and unexplored soil of homosexuals, physically challenged people etc.

Mahesh Dattani has greatly expanded new horizons in Indian English drama. Mahesh Dattani, the most comprehensive dramatic soul born on August 7, 1958 in the city of Bangalore in Karnataka though his parents originally belonged to Porbandar of Gujarat. They migrated to Bombay for business purpose and settled in Bangalore where he found an opportunity of watching Gujarati and Kannada plays.

Dattani took his education from Baldwin High School and St.Joseph College of Arts and Science, Bangalore. Recalling his days at Baldwin, Dattani has a very strong passion for the theatrical art. He longs to present variegated Indian life and sensibility. It is because of these he sets his eyes on the art of the play writing and stage performance.

Mahesh Dattani started his own theatre group named *Playpen* in 1984. It can be interpreted as the manifestation of his abstract ideas and knowledge of art and dance. This *Playpen*, an important performing art group, is very useful for the artist. His plays are performed at his studio. It also encourages the novice artists to participate in dramatic activities.

Mahesh Dattani has given a new height and dimension to Indian English drama. He has rendered great help in bringing out Indian English drama from apologetic existence. Under the patronage of dramatists like Mahesh Dattani, the withering tree of Indian English Drama has started taking its roots and growing rapidly. Besides being the best known dramatist, Dattani is also reputed and accomplished actor, director, scriptwriter and dance teacher.

It has been attributed that Dattani's dramatic art is inspired by the mission to communicate profound meaning through his plays and therefore, he exhibits keen awareness for the direction and stage performance of his own plays. His sensitive dramatic self is a fine synthesis of a dancer, director, actor, and playwright moving collectively towards a single direction.

Dattani has directed and acted in many plays. He performs first in his plays at his Playpen, a theatre company. The plays of other artists are also first performed there and necessary modifications are made in them. Since, Dattani is not a student of any art or literature, the question that what makes him write a play arises in one's mind is his encounter with Gujarati plays is the most significant phenomenon in shaping his mind for theatre business.

Dattani uses Indian words very profusely in his English plays. His characters are fond of using Gujarati dialogues. He has used a good number of Gujarati, Kannada and Hindi words in his plays. Dattani is one of the few dramatist who write their play originally in English. He does not follow western dramatist canons. He has Indianzed his English plays.

With the globalization and arrival of digital technology, the world has become the small global village and English has become the lingua franca of this new global village. He wants to globalize the Indian stage and theatre through his English plays. He has succeeded in making its presence felt at the global level.

Dattanin intends to develop theatre which can be understood and enjoyed by multilingual community of India and abroad. He resorts English as a medium of communication of his theatre. English is a hybrid language and spoken unobtrusively in India. Nevertheless, Dattani puts first transmission of message through performance and secondly transmission of message or ideas through the language of the second.

As a playwright, he has an extraordinary ability to transform his plays into living performance. He has been endowed with the power of perceiving the chemistry of stage. He knows well how to relate his plays to the audience. The function of audience has got much significance in drama. The success of a playwright does not depend only on writing drama text, but entirely depends on its stage ability.

Dattani's plays are dramatic reflections on the concerns and constraints of the commoners. He dramatizes common man's effort to have space and respect in society. He writes about the society and surroundings in which he lives. In this way, his dramatic art is the faithful and authentic expression of his first hand experience and knowledge of socio-cultural environment in which he breathes and lives.

Dattani is a forefront playwright in contemporary Indian Drama in English. He has authored more than one and a half dozen plays differing in themes, tone and treatments. The entire dramatic corpus of Mahesh Dattain's plays can be classified into three categories namely Stage plays, Radio plays and Screen plays.

Dattani has dramatized the problems and issues of the modern urban Indian society ranging from communal tension, homosexuality, child sexual abuse, gender discrimination, marriage and career, conflict between tradition and modernity, patriarchal social system, women, child labourer, interpersonal relationships, workings of personal and moral choices, identity crisis and revelation of the past.

Dattani's *Bravely Fought the Queen is* a bleak play depicting the stunted lives of the members of a joint family and the troubled relationship that dishonesty breeds. The play is set in Bangalore of the 1980s and 1990s and charts the emotional, financial and sexual working in the lives of an urban Indian family of two brothers.

The two brothers are the co-workers of an advertising agency, married to two sisters who mainly remained mostly at home and look after the men's old mother Baa. The play dramatizes the emptiness and shame in the lives of its cloistered women and self-indulgent, unscrupulous men, blurring the lines between fantasy and reality, standing on the brink of terrible secrets, deception and hypocrisies.

Bravely Fought the Queen won the Sahtiya Academic Award on 1998 which shows its uniqueness and greatness. The play deals with three couples, each existing in a hierarchical relation with others. The play centres on the Trivedi family with its two brothers Jiten and Nitin and their wives Dolly and Alka. Jiten exercises control over the family both as an elder son and brother. Dolly and Alka are sisters.

It is a joint family ventures in terms of the domestic scenario as well as the advertising business. All the relations are maintained strictly under some rules and regulations. Praful is the only brother for the two sisters. The third family that intricate with the characters of the Trivedi house is that of Lalitha and Sridhar a couple of whose identity is still in formation.

Jiten the elder son always treats his wife Dolly as a slave. She is considered to be a pawn in his hand. Dolly has been married for fifteen years to Jiten who has always ill-treated and beaten her up. Dolly reminds him up that how on her mother Baa's instigation, he had beaten her up and kicked her when she was pregnant. As a result she gave birth to a premature.

Baa, the mother-in-law keeps filling in the blanks from the upper level that Dolly's brother has lied about their parents. Dolly tells her husband that she did not know what Praful told him about their father and she thought that her husband knows everything before marriage. But the damage was done. At that time Dolly and Alka's father was living with his wife and four children, implying that the two sisters and Praful were born out of wedlock and that their mother was that man's mistress. Baa becomes very angry when she comes to know the truth.

Though Jiten is a womanizer, Dolly never asks him about it and remains silent. Dolly reminds Jiten that she won an argument with him only once and that too when she became pregnant, otherwise it is he who always has his own way. Jiten wants Lalitha to get out of the house before they can argue any further. But Dolly is adamant. She wants to discuss everything with him in Lalitha's presence because she has been a witness to the family's dirty linens washed in the public.

At last when Dolly raises her voice and blames him for everything, at that time he realizes his mistake and apologies to Dolly, blaming Baa for everything that happened. Jiten keeps sobbing and says that Baa made him to do it. But Dolly won't let him get away so easily. She reminds him that he beats and kicks her. Jiten refuses to believe her and rushes out of the main door and move out in car and due to anger he ran his car over the old beggar and woman. In this way both are unable to come to a mutual understanding.

Alka and Nitin consider each other as enemy more than husband and wife. Alka is a spirited young woman in her early thirties and also suffers from the same predicament. But she is gregarious and drowns her sorrow in drink. Jiten never makes any effort to spend time with Alka rather the latter accept some attention from him. That's why when Jiten and Niten planned to take them out both seem to be very euphoric and takes all sort of efforts in order to make themselves gorgeous.

Alka due to curiosity make a call to her husband to ask when they are coming and where they are going in that evening, emphasizing that he was the one who said that they have to go and that too on business matter. Alka is shocked when Niten tells her that the program has been called off. She pleads with him. But Nitin apparently asks her to stay at home and give company to her mother as she is alone.

This really depresses her a lot and feels that her husband does not like her and soon comes to know the truth that her husband is a gay which affects her a lot. It makes Alka to drink in a big way to get over her homosexual husband's neglect and apathy. Nitin on other hand is good looking but meek and timid. He has to be egged on to take actions in this case; he has to be pushed repeatedly by Jiten to drive Alka out of the house but can't bring himself to do so.

Nitin is convinced that he has been tricked into marrying Alka by Praful and he had driven her out of the house earlier when a drunk Alka creates an ugly scene at a family gathering in Praful's presence of cheekily asking Baa whether her two sons as different as chalk is from cheese had the same father. Baa has hated Alka ever since.

Alka's behavior also alienated her brother Praful. He does not visit his sister in town, citing the distance from his hotel to their house. Alka drinks heavily and goes out to drench herself. Soon both the brothers return home and remain dumbstruck with Alka's behavior. Jiten asks Dolly to tell her sister to go inside and change her dress. But Alka does not listen to anyone and make herself busy in drenching in rain.

Soon Nitin goes towards her and ask her to come with him in order to discuss something important. Nitin ask her to look her face in mirror to which Alka says that she knows that she is looking indecent. It is now Jiten's turn to confront his sister-in-law. He turns to Alka and asks her that what she was doing outside in the rain. Alka was obviously acting out of impulse.

Nitin realizes how unfair he has been to Alka and he feels that in order to hide his homosexuality he has been neglecting Alka for a long time. Nitin slowly goes close to Alka, who is asleep on the sofa and speaks to her: "He tricked you too, did not he? How can you still love your brother after what he did to you....? That right. Don't answer just asleep (laughs) you were always a heavy sleeper. Thank god" (BFQ 99-100).

In rest of his monologue, Nitin reveals his homosexual relations with Alka's brother Praful and how he responded to his sexual overtures but makes him ashamed of himself later. At last he accepts Alka as she is with her drunkenness and promiscuity.

In a Joint Hindu family the most intricate relationship is that of the mother-in-law and daughter-in-law. Baa is an old woman who has suffered a stroke. She is confined to bed and alternates between the houses of her sons. Jiten and Niten, whose wives Dolly and Alka look after her by turns. Her loud ringing of the bell and her constant shouting gets on both the sisters nerves and both are equally vehement in getting rid of Baa.

Although irrigating and irksome with her frequent interruptions, Baa emerges as a strong and dominating character in the play. She controls and dictates her daughters-in-law and lives through bullying, blackmailing and instigating one against the other.

Baa never wanted her sons to lead a happy life with their wives and she always makes herself busy in torturing her daughters-in-law and complaining about them to her sons. Dolly tells Baa that she had not gone anywhere but Jiten and Niten will take her and Alka out that evening. Baa asks her whether Praful is coming home to see her. Dolly then comes out with the truth that they are not going out. This show how Baa takes pleasure in each and every minute happening in the life of Alka and Dolly.

Baa watches everything that is happening in her sons' home and refuses to give the house to Nitin despite his pleadings. She has appointed Praful as the trustee to her property as she has seen how fond Pranful is of her grand-daughter. She is very keen to see Praful in order to expiate her past sins and also to entrust Daksha to his care.

Praful comes across as a caring individual although he has been Nitin's lover in the past and both Nitin and Alka can't forgive him for having tricked them into their loveless and childless marriage. According to Baa it is only

Praful who loves Daksha, her own blood; she is convinced that only Praful can look after her spastic grand-daughter to whom, she has willed her house with Praful as the trustee.

In India it is generally considered that the love between the mother and son to be pure, divine and true but in this play it is fully tops turvey as both mother and sons use each other in order to fulfill their own desire and to take revenge on others. Jiten and Nitin's father was a cruel and a dark man who harassed their mother. This kind of cruelty perpetrated on Baa by her husband is brought to light every now and then in the play when she feels jittery even after so many years of his death.

Baa sees the picture of her husband in her elder son, Jiten and thus automatically develops an inclination towards her younger son, Nitin who resembles her a lot. Nitin is more subdued and sympathetic character. In the childhood itself Nitin always supported his mother as he openly says that he hates his father and ask him to go away and takes his mother in his protective arms.

Baa really takes a lot of care for Nitin and that's why she rejects him not to marry Alka but even then he marries her and goes against his mother, which hurts her a lot. She thinks that Alka is trying to take her son away from her due to which she always adds fuel to fire when Nitin is angry with his wife. Baa even force him to throw her out of their house which he can't be able to do as he seem to have little bit love for her that too because he loved her brother.

Jiten knows the fact that his mother loves his brother more than himself that's why when they are in desperate need of money for the business, Jiten eggs on Nitin, Baa's favourite son, to will the house to him. This would take care of their financial problems without having recourse to Praful's money that he has generously offered them. He asks him to throw Alka out of the house in order impress her but Nitin failed to do so.

When Jiten moves forward to ask for the property before that his mother asks what he wants from her and says that she wants to meet Prayful, who is the trustee of the house and she has willed the house to Daksha. This was really shock news for Nitin and Baa adds that she knows that no one loves Daksha and may be Jiten loves his daughter but she does not love him. Nitin who has all along considered himself Baa's favourite son.

Keeping Baa alternately in their houses and tending to her needs is a chore each one of them hates. Jiten is only interested in his mother's property which he wants Nitin to get willed in his name before Baa dies. Jiten considers his mother to be a sentimental fool as she mostly lives in her past after she has had a stroke.

The relationships between the brothers are not good. They never respected any relation in their life from their mother to wife. Jiten and Nitin are as different as chalk is from cheese. Jiten is hugem reckless and violent. Nitin on the other hand is good looking but meek. Both of them run an advertising agency they have taken over from a man who owned them money.

Jiten and Nitin always take disadvantage of Praful's excess love and care for his sister. They badly need the prestigious account, but the prevailing interest rated in the market is exorbitant and prohibitive. But Jiten asks Nitin not to worry as the sentimental fool Praful has offered them an interest free loan of ten lakhs.

Jiten says that when it comes to his sister, he will do anything for them and asks Nitin not to let Alka to know about it and he will handle Dolly. Although Nitin is against this, he eventually agrees and forces Jiten to ask for twelve lakhs in a day are two, so that they can circulate the extra two lakhs on interest.

Pranful brother-in-law and mother are against him, but he wants to help them just for the sake for his sister's happy life. This shows the immense love towards his sister. When Praful visited his sister Alka was fully drunk and insulted her husband and mother-in-law who further humiliated Praful for not teaching good manners to Alka which hurts him a lot. Alka replies that she was angry with him and wanted to make him feel small and considers her brother as a cheat who lied about their father to them and he even lied to Alka by not telling the truth that Nitin is a homosexual.

The relationship between the two sisters is also not good, although Praful sends them to same home as daughters-in-law with the hope that both will support each other, but everything turns opposite. It is Dolly who always takes care of Alka but Alka always finds the situation to taunt her by talking about her daughter and her ignorance.

Even when Alka is planned to throw out by Nitin and Baa, Dolly is the only soul to beg and fight with her husband to protect Alka at each and every situation. But Alka never feels the real love of her sister and even fights with her for not telling the cancellation of the program that they planned to go on that evening. Dolly tries to justify the truth that she herself does not know about this but her sister does not believe in her.

Dolly forgets the fight soon, but it is Alka who teases her that at parties her sister just sits in the corner sipping her lime juice and speaks when spoken to. She refuses to mix refuses to be interesting and that's why they don't take us out more often. Dolly bickers with Alka, who has only been married for two years, already claiming that she has a better deal than her in marriage.

Alka cautions her not to bring other things into the argument since they are talking about socializing and she must stick to it. Sensing that she has gone too far in her thought, Dolly concedes that her sisters is right and agree that she must learn to be a bit more sociable, adding tongue in cheeks and admits that she is not half as talkative as Alka and asks Lalitha some tips.

Lalitha is keen to ingratiate herself with Dolly and Alka because she wants the Re Va Tee deal to come through. This would immensely help Sridhar in his profession. She tells the two sisters how she keeps herself occupied by making occupied by making bonsai and even gifts a fully grown miniature tree with small organs to Dolly.

The secret of growing a healthy bonsai is to trim it from time to time and stunt its growth-something Dolly and Alka's husbands have not done in their case. They have been left to their own devices by their husbands. The bonsai is thus a symbol of the sisters stunted growth, leading to indifference and general disinterestedness in Dolly who is forever lost in Naina Devi's thumris and Alka who has taken to drink in a big way.

Both the sisters are bitchy and do not miss a chance to have a dig at each other. Alka needing Dolly about Daksha and the replacement of cook Kanhaiya and Dolly reveling in Alka's misdemeanors which are a perpetual source of embarrassment to the family. Lalitha, who relishes playing one sister against the other and then trying to act as the peace-maker.

The sisters release comes in the form of Lalitha and her presentation of a bonsai tree with orange fruits to Dolly and Alka, whose growth and development has been stunned and dwarfed by their husband's and Baa's domination of their lives.

In this whole play only Sridhar and Lalitha prove to be an embodiment of a couple. Throughout the play both of them remain as a support to each other emotionally and professionally. Lalitha seems to take full interest in her husband's job and always thinks for its development day and night.

Sridhar and his wife Lalitha are devoted to growing bonsais and presenting them to those whose favours they seek. But self interest weights above everything else for the ambitious couple, they are ready to stoop to any level to further interests. Sridhar suffers humiliation in order to save his job. But when it comes to his wife he shows his real love and support only for her. Nitin when shouts at Lalitha and asks her to get out of his home.

Sridhar crosses to Jiten takes his glass and throws its contents on Jiten's face. He gets up and grabs Sridhar by the throat, Sridhar kicks about and beats him, but is over-powered by Jiten's bulk and violence. Jiten threatens him that if he shows his face in his office again, he will kill him. This really hurts the husband and wife a lot and Sridhar makes up his mind that where his wife is not given any respect he will not work there anymore.

Sridhar now has made up his mind that he would handle the Re Va Tee account on his own and leaves the place. As he can't work in the place where his wife is not at all respected. Since he has decided to break free from the bothers' grip he finally decides to punish him for all his cruelty.

The bonsai-loving Lalitha and her husband have largely been the audience, sometimes catalysts and at times active participants in the affairs of the Trivedi family. Initially they relish the position they are placed in, but gradually realize that they are being treated like crap. The last straw is Jiten's insulting behavior towards Lalitha.

The bonsai motif stands for the growth, the dwarfed maturity and unrealized potential of at least three characters in the play-Dolly, Alka and Sridhar. They confront and get over their problems and the stumbling blocks in their way by standing up for their rights. Each fight his or her own battle in the manner she or he deems fit. The bonsai in symbolizes the fact that unlike in Ibsen's plays, the human spirit is not crushed at the end of Dattani's play.

Dattani's play simply asks one question to the audience that why the society do demands faithfulness of a woman to her husband but not the faithfulness of a man to his wife. Alka is all armed to fight back and question the norms set by men for women and Dolly is ready to join her.

Dattani shows clearly how joint family is breaking down in our society. All the traditional values are thrown into wind. Man and women became individualistic, selfish, and self centred. Like John Arden, Dattani writes Kitchen sink plays which make us aware of the contemporary reality. In fact, social realism is an important aspect of Dattani's play.

In *Dance like a Man*, Jairaj and Ratna seemed to be living with Jairaj's father named Amritlal who has full control over the family and always wanted his son to be under his own control and never wanted his son to be a dancer which was the ambition of Jairaj. Jairaj follows his heart's desire and becomes a dancer but has enraged his father in this process. Amritlal upholds the traditional values, whereas his son Jairaj, seeks to overthrow it through his course of action.

Throughout the play, the old man and his son appears to be living in the different worlds without any interaction. Amritlal is an autocratic father who does not try to understand the emotions, the aspirations and the problems of his own son. He does not like his son's passion towards dance. The father pursues the traditional values, whereas the son tracks the modern outlook.

Jairaj's daughter Lata is an aspiring and promising young dancer. She is a great talented girl who is greatly affected by the thwarted ambitions and frustrations of her parent's youth and expectations they place upon her. Through Lata, her parents struggle to keep the art form alive. The play forms a link between three generations.

Now-a-days this theme becomes more important due to rapid industrialization, and the westernization of attitudes and lives of the people. D.H. Lawrence points out that the great relationship for humanity will always be the relationship between man and woman. The relation between man and man, woman and woman, parent and child will always subsidiary. (D.H. Lawrence 130).

Family is not only an important constituent of Indian society but the nerve centre of Indian life. Mahesh Dattani examines the relationship among the members of the family with accuracy and authenticity. Family relationship can be defined as the way in which a person is related to somebody else in the family. How they behave towards each other, how they affect each other, or how they are similar to each other, all this falls within the ambit of a family relationship.

The play *Dance Like a Man,* a stage play in two acts, is one of the most wonderful dramatic creations of Mahesh Dattani. The stage performance of the play has earned a critical acclaim in India and abroad. In this play, Dattani explores pathos of human predicament in the subtlest way. It embodies a brilliant study of human relationships as well as human weaknesses.

The play depicts the clash between issues such as marriage, career and the place of a woman in patriarchal social set up. It deals with the lives of the people who feel exhausted and frustrated on account of the hostile surroundings and unfavorable circumstances. The story is unfolded in time past and time present.

The play encapsulates their present tension and past struggle as well as their present efforts and past discontentment. They reflect upon their past struggle, success and failures as the dancers. This unveils seeming harmony between the two and puts forth a marriage discord and domestic conflict that forms the substance of the play. The opening scene of the play provides important information about all the people of the play and their social and family background.

Amritlal does not like his daughter-in-law Ratna learning the art of dance with the association of devdasi. He fears of his family reputation being spoiled. He also thinks that they have nothing to do with their art. But Jairaj has high regard and respects for them and their art. Amritlal has no heart for art. He speaks about art very contemptuously. He forbids Jairaj mixing with other dancers. The clash between the father and son symbolizes the clash between tradition and modernity.

Amritlal was a loving father as he makes arrangements for his son's dance but he cannot adjust himself with the ideas that his son wants to adopt dancing as a profession. Family name and social recognition are the chief concerns for Amritlal Parekh, but for his son Jairaj, they are the obstacle in carving his self identity. He yields but does not kill his own desire. He craves for self identity and self esteem.

In the society everyone wants the male to earn that much so that the house would run properly but Amritlal knew that dance would not help Jairaj to earn enough money and that would make him unworthy in the eyes of his wife Ratna. For Amritlal, dance was good as far as it remains a hobby but it was not proper to be taken as a profession.

Jairaj and his wife Ratna leaves the house as a protest against the traditional notions and restrictions imposed upon them by Amritlal. Jairaj makes himself free from the clutches of his autocratic father. He does not want to stay even a minute further and resolves to never set foot in the house again. They go away throwing old restrictions to the wind. His determination and tenacity to adhere to what he wishes to do compel him to leave the house.

Jairaj have realized that the house of their autocratic father is better than the world that exists outside. After two days, he returns back to his father's house. He never makes a compromise with the state of affairs knuckling under the power of his father who exploits the situation to curtail Jairaj's individual freedom. However he continues to hate his father's guts till the end of the story.

After his father's death, he removes the gardening to show his hatred for his father. Thus the relation between the son and father shows a crucial one as it focuses on the question of inherited values and assumptions. It becomes a microcosm of the debate between the generations.

Jairaj suffers in two ways. Firstly, patriarchal power suppresses his desires and dreams. Secondly, social prejudice also causes turmoil and suffering in the life of Jairaj. So, his self is divided and pride is wounded. He is anguished and depressed. Critically speaking, the play is a tragedy of human soul. Jairaj's soul falls to pieces. He is constantly shown at war. The shift in past shows his clash with his father and in present, he is struggling to adjust with his wife. He expresses his grievances against his father and wife.

Ratna loses her faith in Jairaj and she is no longer proud of her husband after Jairaj's return to his ancestoral abode. Her passion for dance makes her to go to extend of betraying her husband when she assures her father in law of trying her level best to help him grow up.

At that time it is realized that Ratna is an ambitious lady. Dance is her dream and soul. She marries Jairaj only for the reason that he will allow her to dance. Behind, all her moves in the drama, dance became the main factor. Her character has a negative shade. She follows her heart overpowered by mind and tries to be famous using dance as a medium.

Throughout the play Jairaj appears as one who suffers on account of choosing his own path. His portrayal is so noble that he never blames Ratna for the death of their son Shankar that was the result of her carelessness. Opposite to general understanding or expectation here Amritlal tries to control Jairaj's passion for traditional dance and for that takes her help. This play witnesses the psychological manipulation of a man by his wife and father.

Amritlal also tries to control the movement and manners of Ratna. In this way, the clash between the tradition and the modernity is heightened through the conflict between Amritlal and Ratna. Amritlal knows that Ratna is going to visit a *devdasi* instead of going to temple.

The play shows how patriarchal social set up deprives the other members of the families from being celebrity as a dancer. Ratna couldn't be a famous dancer under the patriarchal powers exercised by her father-in-law. Dattani seems to assert that individual talent can never flourish under the domination of patriarchal family system. Ratna thwarts in her dream of being celebrity. After the death of Amritlal Parekh, her daughter Lata has become an excellent star of *bharatnatyam.*

Dattani wants to depict the society that a father should not remain as a barrier in the path of their son's ambition and moreover the parents must not force their aims and desires on their children. If a man or woman fails to identify himself or herself with the spouse, marriage becomes hellish. There must be strong bond of relationship between the husband and wife. They must overcome all sorts of problems in their life.

In the play *Dance Like a Man*, Dattani examines interpersonal human relationship within the range of familial territory. The theme of clash between tradition and modernity has already been assessed by a number of authors, but Dattani has provided a variety and vividness to this theme. *Dance Like a Man* has been hailed as wonderful and engrossing play.

The play displays its deep concern for family harmony and approach for a social reformation, which makes it a unique piece of art. The play ends with a compromising tone. They survive by making compromise with their revolutionary and rebellious spirit.

Dance Like a Man has been hailed as wonderful and engrossing play. The play displays its deep concern for family harmony and approach for a social reformation, which makes it a unique piece of art. The play ends with a compromising tone. They survive by making compromise with their revolutionary and rebellious spirit. The play ends with following memorable words: "We were only human. We lacked the grace. We lacked the brilliance. We lacked the magic to dance like God." (DLM: 447)

Tara is the most touching three-act stage play by Dattani. The play revolves around the theme of favoring the boy and frowning upon the girl with exceptional originality of conception. The playwright presents arguments against the parents' preference for the male child at the cost of girl child. The play holds much significance in the present time especially when the government and other NGO's are holding programmes and rallies for creating awareness among people against female foeticide.

Mahesh Dattani's *Tara* comes across as a play that deals with twin aspects that are two sides of the same coin. It also presents the conflict between illusion and reality as echoed by the multi-level set. The house of the Patels is kept as if in memory. The only realistic level is the part of the wall covered with faded wall paper that has the writer writing the play in which he appears to the audience.

In this sense, the playwright presents Meta theatrical aspects as he talks of distancing oneself from the experience and writing about it. The Doctor as portrayed in the set stands in contrast as the omnipotent Author. It thereby underlines the clash between the subjective and objective author. Chandan discovers that even distancing himself physically in a seedy suburb of London thousands of miles away from home hasn't done the trick.

He attempts as much as possible to alienate himself from the script, but suffers from a writer's block and everything remains stagnant on his paper just as his life is. Just as in his life, nothing changes but the dates. And the greatest irony is that Indo-Anglian literature isn't worth toilet paper in his own country. He neglects his own personal history to get over his guilt with what happened to Tara.

Just as the lowest portion occupies a major portion of the stage, the memory of guilt haunts and dominates Chandan's personality. It is to deny this that he creates his alter-ego Dan. His being a Diaspora, this causes another divide in his self: the identity of the Diaspora caught between his native culture and foreign culture as signified by Chandan and Dan.

Tara circles around the grave and traditional issues of gender bias. The son and daughter delivered from same womb are preferentially treated by no less than parents themselves in the intoxication of superstition and ancestral beliefs and the daughter is sacrificed for the short term benefit of the son. The play is contextual and relevant in the light of the increasing incidents of foeticide, infanticide and widening gap in the sex ratio of male and female child.

In the play, Tara is the daughter of an educated higher middle class family in Banglore. The story of the play is about the twins who are born with three legs and blood supply to the third leg is from the baby girl's body. Only one of the twins could have two legs, and the other had to survive with only one leg. It is decided to fix the third leg on to the male baby's body so as to make male baby complete. This decision was not on the basis of medical ground but due to gender discrimination in our society.

Mahesh Dattani has very deftly dealt with the fate awaiting the girl child. The social norms, economic standards and cultural factors have been responsible for the injustice against the girl child. All these factors combine to create the social system in which the girl child has to live and die. Tara is killed by this social system, which controls the minds and actions of the people. The trauma of coming to know the role her mother had played in her life, and the discrimination becomes too much for her. Tara`s potentiality was sacrificed at the altar of gender.

The childhood and Indian name of Dan is Chandan. Dan is both the narrator and character of the drama and spectators watch the drama from the points of view of Dan so it is called Dan's play. He is deemed as the Sutradhar of the play. All the actions and characterizations pertaining to drama are portrayed through revelation made by Dan and most of the actions in the drama are resulting from the flash back of Patel's family six years earlier.

The play, Tara opens with Dan who remains busy in typing the text pertaining to his lifelong experience. Dan is undergoing mental pain and conflict caused by reverberation of some tragic incidents of the past. Dan and Tara had shared one body which is popularly and scientifically known as Siamese twins and in the terms of Dan they were like two lives and one body, in one comfortable womb.

He lives in London to keep sufficient distance between his bruised past and present. A play within the play is witnessed as Dan is writing a script of a drama known as "Twinkle Tara" which has comprehensive connotation as Tara is protagonist of the drama under discussion and also the literal meaning of the twinkling star.

The play suddenly takes the shape of flashback and action suddenly moves back towards Mumbai where Dan and Tara had passed their childhood lives. The scene of traditional, patriarchal and paradigmatic Indian family is observed wherein Bharati, the mother of Tara and Dan just finishes her worship and Patel, the father of the twin, is getting ready to join his duty.

Both Bharati and Patel seem to be in the milieu of making Chandan a writer and Tara, as usual, strong, healthy and beautiful to be a belle bride of the future. Bharati and Patel belong to two different states, Karnataka and Gujarat respectively and they were not in good terms and always shown to be quarreling with each other owing to cultural gap and dominance and intervention of Bharati's father in the relationship of Bharati and Patel.

Dr. Thakkar is bribed by Bharati's father to operate the Siamese Twin according to his wish and thus he earns notoriety to the name and fame of doctor who is deemed as next to godliness for healing the wounds and pains of the aggrieved and diseased. Father-in-law of Patel has played a villainous role in this play and he is responsible for the imbroglios, gender bias and class discrimination encountered by Patel's family.

It is he who bribes Dr. Thakkar to carry out surgery in favour of Chandan. He is of belief that male should always be given golden opportunity and his penchant for male chauvinism remains unabated when he left money for only his grandson, Chandan and nothing for Tara. Dattani aptly demonstrates that how the interventions of in-laws into the family affairs destroy its smooth functioning, harmony and cordial atmosphere.

Bharati's father is responsible for bringing bitterness between her and her husband, Patel. Though it is another thing Patel should not have remained mute onlooker to the discrimination perpetuated on Tara by Bharati and her father. He is further an accomplice in the malicious acts of gender bias when he chalks out plans for a better education and career of Chandan.

The title 'Tara' is symbolic of a shooting star that is a temporary guest of a small fraction of time as the protagonist is. The idea also brings to mind the concept of the Binary star systems that consist of two stars that are gravitationally bound, and generally move around each other in stable orbits.

When two such stars have a relatively close orbit, their gravitational interaction can have a significant impact on their evolution. Just as the Siamese twins in this case have an interwoven identity; and has a great impact on each other, mentally and biologically in their evolution. They are spiritually inseparable.

With the demise of Tara, Chandan experiences a sense of identity crisis. The inseparable twins very evocatively remind us of the celebrated pair Rahel and Estha in Arundhati Roy's *The God of Small Things* who are forcibly separated by choice. Just as they emerge from a zygote they get back their revenge on society as they go into a taboo method of fusion towards the end of the novel.

The twins in the prescribed play are born as 'inseparably fused'-hugging each other emblematizing their emotional coherence at the very outset. Chandan envisages their reconciliation towards the end of the play as they get together in a tight embrace, back to their former fused form. They stand for two sides of the same concept.

Dattani sees *Tara* as a play about the gendered self, about coming to terms with the feminine side of oneself in a world that favours always what is 'male'. The quality of being effeminate is a reason for shame in India. The playwright also seeks to portray science and nature in a similar manner. How Science and Nature complement each other. However Science cannot conquer everything and has its own lapses as Nature does.

This is signified by the twins with impaired legs as they form a mirror image of each other. The play depicts how Science cannot always conquer Nature as the leg attributed to the boy is rejected by the body in a brash attempt at disregarding both Nature and God. Dan hits the nail on the head when he asserts Conflict is the crux of life.

A duel to death between God and nature on one side and on other the amazing Dr.Thakkar.(330)This explains the God-like stance of the Doctor, who is seated with a seeming omnipotent presence representing Advanced Technology. Behind, on a higher level, is a chair in which Dr.Thakkar remains seated throughout the play. Although he doesn't watch the action of the play, his connection is asserted by his Sheer God-like presence.(323)

The drama has two sides to it with respect to the time frame-the past and the present. It also reflects the virtual and the real. An utterance sometimes refers to two different time frames with respect to time, occasion and the statement applicable to different characters. The following lines hold true for both Bharati and Dan as they are distant in time and space: "If at all they must know, it will be from me. Not from you. "(345)

The twins, especially 'Tara', are repeatedly referred to as "freaks". The term 'freak' has been conventionally used to refer to person who has something unusual regarding their appearance or behaviour. The older usage of the word 'freaks' refers to the state of being physically deformed, or characterized by rare diseases and conditions.

The word was utilized to suggest 'sideshow performers'. In such an instance, the word 'freak' represents the state of Women, who are marginalized. The female race who are not congenitally deformed but are so as society forces the handicap upon them. Just as it is presented in concrete terms in the play: Tara's leg is callously separated from her to render her twin brother normal, defying the tenets of Nature.

It echoes Simone de Beauvoir's dictum:" "One is not born a woman, one becomes one." A natural freak refers to a genetic abnormality, while a made freak is a once normal person who experienced or initiated an alteration at some point in life (such as receiving surgical implants). Here both the terms can be used to describe Dan and Tara.

But Tara is less of a natural freak; as Nature was more in her favour. "Freak" has also been employed to describe genetic mutations in plants and animals, i.e. "freaks of nature"."Freak" used in the verb form, implies: "to become stressed and upset". Here, the twins are in a state of depression owing to their predicament but utilize a curtain of sarcasm and wit to shield the same.

Man cannot accept the woman's intellect, and gets intimidated by her intelligence. Tara's victory at the card game is seen as thorough cheating and Chandan is ashamed to admit her victory. He sees her as a good business woman as she cheats at cards; not attributing it to her business acumen, but to her shrewdness.

Tara gets hurt at the remark as it holds no truth value. Even Patel ignores her future prospects and the need to engage her in any meaningful Endeavour. She is forced to conform to the stereotype of the Indian Woman-devoid of any intellect, deemed fit only to perform mechanical household chores. In other words, a domestic animal, which can be cared for, but not regarded with respect.

Tara quips at this: "The men in the house were deciding on whether they were going hunting while the women looked after the cave."(328) She highlights the plight of women who were presumed to be suitable for the domestic domain only.

The play as a whole thus depicts the relegation of the relevance of the Woman, and her upper edge whenever it does assert itself in a male-dominated society. This is why the Grandfather and the Mother who represent tradition prefer the male over the female; the Male is the archetypal successor or prototype of cultural progeny.

This explains why the author names the play after the female child whose identity is demoted otherwise; in order to invert the dialectical pair male/female. The woman has always been hailed in philosophy, but in practice she is treated as an object to be overlooked.

In the play, though Bharati dotes on her daughter Tara, she insensitively attributes a piece of her daughter to the son. The conflict between illusion and reality is yet again echoed here. What is actually a public display of attention on part of the mother is actually a screen to shield her guilt. The context also serves as a satire on the self-sufficient Indian male, for whom, to accept anything feminine is beneath his dignity, and an indelible question mark on his masculinity.

Even Dan acknowledges the same, as he writes the play. Though the craft of the play is his, he has to borrow the material from Tara. In *Tara*, the deformity of the Woman is caused by the Man, and caused in order to complete the Man. The playwright utilizes the motif symbolically as well. This is the reason why Tara approaches her end more quickly, and it is not owing to her inferiority.

The handicap also symbolizes the predicament of girls in Indian families who are made to forsake their chances of getting educated as the edification of the boy becomes a priority. The death of Tara has a more powerful impact than her existence. Just as the death of the Star gives way to the Black Hole.

The Black Hole stands for the God in the World of Physics, it being linked to the Male Gods in Hinduism like Shiva, Krishna, Ram etc. who are black. Religion has also been predominantly patriarchal. Christianity professes. By naming his female protagonist as 'Tara', Mahesh Dattani puts it otherwise.

The play *Thirty Days in September dramatizes* theme of child sexual abuse within the range of familial relationship, whereas *The Swami and Winston* also deals with the mystery of murder of English lady. Here Uma Rao, again, unveils the curtain from the murder mystery of English lady. The dramatist exposes psuedo and scheming scholars in this play. Like afore said two plays, *Uma and Fairy Queen* is also a detective in nature.

The play *A Tale of a Mother Feeding Her Child* is a very interesting and enchanting radio play. The first broadcasting of the play was done on October 29, 2000 on BBC Radio. Mahesh Dattani was commissioned to write plays for BBC Radio on the occasion of six hundredth anniversary of Geoffrey Chaucer. This play was written for this purpose.

The play dramatizes the journey of English lady Anna Gosweb to an Indian village after twenty years to meet and help her drought stricken boy friend Jaman. Unfortunately, her friend Jaman dies before she reaches his village.

The play *Clearing the Rubble* is a very brief but touching radio play. It depicts the misery and malady of earth quake affected people of Kutch region in Gujarat. *Morning Raga* is his famous screen play. It is based on life of Swarnlatha, a carnatic singer. The play is greatly appreciated for its music as motif.

The play presents dexterously emotional turmoil in the lives of the various characters of the play. Dattani observes: It is about a meeting of two worlds. A story that brings together the modern and the traditional unites the past with the present, Carnatic music with Western music, fate and coincidence with individual choices.

The play *Ek Alag Mausam* is dramatic achievement of Mahesh Dattani. It deals with the serious issue of human life. The dramatist tries to articulate the voice of the marginalized being HIV positives through this play. Like post-colonial writers, Dattani attempts to seek the space for the HIV positives in the society. He reflects the ethos of the subaltern section of our society.

The play depicts post modernistic theme-love story of two HIV positives. The play lays bare their love for life. The play has two layers of ideas; need for the creation of social awareness against HIV and love and understanding for the HIV afflicted.

In this way, Mahesh Dattani makes daring efforts to depict quite unconventional and radical themes in his plays. The complexities of human relationship and predicament of the modern men find due expression in his dramatic works. His dramatic techniques and stagecraft are superb.

There are rapid shifts in terms of time and space. He has made use of different images, symbols, devices, techniques etc. to communicate his ideas in a very effective and concrete manner. Dattani's theatrical genious is characterized by diversity, dynamism, and innovative urge. He is an unconventional voice in the theatrical firmament of India. He seeks to present volcanic dimensions of rage and resentment as well as distrust and discontent shrouded inside the psychological domain of human consciousness.

Dattani's theatrical creed asserts that human nature has its own autonomous space. Any act of encroachment to this space, either through conventional ideology or by any other means, will result into agitation and uprising causing chaos and destruction.

Mahesh Dattani is the most powerful dramatist in the present Indian English dramatic world. He has enriched and embellished tradition of Indian Drama with his experiments and innovations. With the arrival of Mahesh Dattani on the literary scene, the scenario begins to change. His plays are originally written in English. He has authored a good number of dramas diverse in themes, techniques and devices. Moreover, his plays have been produced on the stage very successfully.

Dattani's plays are dramatic reflections on the anxiety and restraints of the commoners. He dramatizes common man's efforts to have space and respect in society. He writes about the society and surroundings in which he lives. In this way, his dramatic art is the faithful and authentic expression of his first hand experience and knowledge of socio-cultural environment in which he breathes and lives.

His presentation of problems from real life situations is significant contribution to Indian English Drama. Among modern Indian playwrights, he stands forth with singular distinctness, striking artistic perception, and immense dramatic guts. He is the most serious contemporary dramatist in Indian drama in English. He takes up serious problems existing in urban India. His plays contain some important elements like human pathos, passions, conflict and appeal to human sentiment, which can immediately touch and stir common audience.

4. ASIF CURRIMBHOY

Among all the playwrights of the Post Independence era, the most prolific playwright is Asif Currimbhoy. He has been called India's first authentic voice in the theatre. He is among those few dramatists whose plays have been successfully staged in India as well as abroad. He has published more than thirty plays within the period of eighteen years beginning in 1959.

He has shown a deep concern in producing drama. His plays are appreciated outside India. Unlike other dramatists, Asif's plays are meant for the stage. He brilliantly succeeds in producing actable plays which have given international reputation to him.

The range and variety of his themes are wide. He has worked over the issues related to history, politics, socioeconomic problems and conflicts, religion, psychological conflicts, east west encounter, philosophy and art. K.R.S. Iyengar in his academic discourse appreciates Currimbhoy Farce, comedy, melodrama, tragedy, history, fantasy: Currimbhoy handles them all with commendable ease.

Born in 1928, Asif belongs to a family of industrialists who were distinguished by the British government in the field of industry. His father was a liberal minded intellectual and his mother was a social worker. Both deeply influenced Asif in his teenage. He was brought up in an environment of education and innovative ideas which formed an integral part of his temperament later in his life.

His school period also had an impact over his literary output. He studied at Xavier"s high school, Bombay and pursued his higher education at

Wisconsin University. It gave exposure to the English language and to some extent to western culture.

Though he studied in a Christian missionary school, he did not keep himself away from the Indian culture. He made a thorough study of the *Bhagvad Gita* and the *Upnishads* and also the Hindu epics like The *Ramayana* and The *Mahabharata*. The impact of this study can be seen in his works.

After schooling in India, he went to the United States for college studies and spent four years there. He studied at Winsconsin University before graduating from the University of California in Economics in 1950. He recalls his experiences in the University in U.S.A. College was in America, those beautiful mid-west landscapes of snow and loneliness.

The love for language and life grew and in isolation of a groping search and hyper sensitivity. As a University student, he loved and admired Shakespeare. He visited different dramatic productions and was very well aware of the various trends in drama in the U.S.A. all this contributed in making him a man of theatre.

Currimbhoy was motivated for writing by his wife Suraiya whom he married soon after he returned to India. The major incidents which took place in sixties influenced Currimbhoy. Independence to India led to the partition of the country which caused the anguish in all over the nation but especially in Bengal and Punjab. Currimbhoy was deeply influenced by the violence prevailing in the country and the condition of people in those days.

Asif got several opportunities to visit different places in all over the world and observe them keenly. He joined the New India Assurance Company in 1954 through which he came in contact with French culture. Soon he left the New India Assurance Company and joined Burmah-Shell in

India. As a marketing executive he toured throughout India and came in contact with different locales and various problems of the people.

From this, it is clear that Currimbhoy is a keen observer of people and particularly their mode of expression. All these influences left an impression on his literary output. He began writing in his late twenties. The literary career of Asif Currimbhoy can be divided into two periods, the first period ranging from 1959 to 1968 and the second period from 1969 to 1975.

During the first period he wrote *The Tourist Mecca* (1959), *The Clock* (1959), *The Restaurant* (1960), *The Dumb Dancer* (1961), *OM* (1961), *Thorns on a Canvas* (1962), *The Captives* (1963), *Goa* (1964), *And Never the Twain Shall Meet* (1964), *The Kaleidoscope* (1964), *Monsoon* (1965), *The Hungry Ones* (1965), *Valley of the Assassins* (1966), *The Temple Dancers* (1967), *The Lotus Eater* (1967), *Abbe Faria* (1968), and *The Mercenary* (1968).

In the second period, he wrote *An Experiment with Truth* (1969), *The Great Indian Bustard* (1970), *Inquilab* (1970), *Darjeeling Tea?* (1971), *The Refugee* (1971), *Sonar Bangla* (1972), *Om Mane Padme Hum!* (1972), *The Miracle Seed* (1973), *Angkor* (1973), *The Dissident MLA* (1974), and *This Alien... Native Land* (1975). Out of these he did not publish *The Restaurant, And Never the Twain Shall Meet, The Kaleidoscope, Monsoon, The Temple Dancers, The Lotus Eater, The Mercenary* and *The Great Indian Bustard*.

His plays are inspired by some incidents or situations, he observed in his surroundings or experienced himself. In 1958, he was posted to Agra where he had to spend his time in drinking sessions at hotels. He wrote *Tourist Mecca* which deals with the tourists to Agra. It was during his stay in Agra when he faced some problems in his job and his inner tension found expression in the play *The Clock*.

The play *The Doldrummers* portrays the lives of the youth living on the Juhu Beach. He might have inspired for this play during his visits on Juhu Beach for holidays and weekends. He made a thorough study of Indian mythology and Indian philosophy. He wrote *The Dumb Dancer* and *OM* which are influenced by Indian myth and philosophy.

The Dumb Dancer is a psychological play based on the theme from *The Mahabharata* and *OM* reflects the playwright's obsession with the fear of death. *Thorns on a Canvas* was written due to the banning of *The Dold rummers* as it expresses the bitter experience of the playwright. The play *The Captives* takes up the issue of Indo-Chinese conflict of October 1962 but actually it probes into the human psyche after the partition.

The *Dumb Dancer* is the study of a Kathakali dancer who tries to identify himself with Bhima. It is a dance play from the episode of 'The Slaughter of Duryodhana' in the ancient epic of Mahabharata. The play moves through the dancer's confused mind as he hovers between reality and the world of myth. In the words of Paul Verghese it goes to the credit of Asif Currimbhoy that he had made the Kathakali dance an integral part of the play.

Asif Currimbhoy shows great craftsmanship in characterization and uses psycho-analysis to probe into the complexities, tensions and frustrations of his characters. Here, Dr Prema is not presented just as psychiatrist only but as a full-blooded human being who grows and develops with the advancement of the play. The Dumb Dancer' is a play of suspense shrouded in myth and involving a lot of psycho-analysis from the beginning to end.

The play has its roots in the dim past of Hinduism. He describes starvations and famines and never ignores the lot of the poor. There is enough of bloodshed in his plays like Inquilab, The refugee and Sonar

Bangla but can he help it? Not at all! He portrays these goary scenes faithfully, not to give us enjoyment but rather to bring to our senses.

He accepts that war is a tragedy and feels pinched why others don't think in the same way. He constantly gives us a feeling that the voice of sanity is lost in the din of unreason. He is seemingly so dispassionate and neutral about the situations and events that no one dare doubt his integrity.

Asif Currimbhoy is no more in this world but his monumental works remain which continuously spread his fame and name throughout the entire English-speaking world. His plays are displayed throughout the European countries. Hundreds of critics have taken interest in his dramatic art and literary journals are often publishing articles about his art. Such luminaries as Edward Said, Faubian Bowers and Fanon worked on his dreams, Peter Nazareth wrote about him as a dramatist of public event.

In India his own people did not lack behind in evaluating his dramatic acumen. Srinivasa, Professor Iyanger, Prof. Sunil Dutta and Paul Verghese exploited the different aspects of his art. Looking through his eyes, the prevailing conditions concerning economical and social life of India towards the end of 21st century are to be guessed well. His dramas can humanize the population of the subcontinent.

His Social and Semi-romantic dramas will be dealt with separately, describing old love adventures which cut across all social bindings. Detailed analysis will enable us to lay thread-bare the backdrop of Asif Currimbhoy's dramas and give a true picture of causes and events which formed the base of his plays. Asif Currimbhoy got a job in New India Assurance Company in Paris which brought him in touch with French culture also.

Later, he joined the Burma Shell in India wherein he worked as an executive. This caused him to travel throughout India extensively and enabled him to familiarize himself with people and customs of different regions and localities. This great exposure, more especially to experimental American theatre, as well as his vivid interest in history led him to compose such monument a plays showing his great engagement with life.

Inquilab focuses on Prof. Datta who finds his students resorting to violence propounded by the Marxists. Datta finds it impossible to continue persuading his students with Gandhian ideals. His son Amar ties to convince him of the Marxist ideologies when he affirms. The revolution takes its toll, Datta is killed by his own elder son who is a Naxal extremist.

Jain the landlords is another victim of violence. Finally Amar comes to the realization that his father was right in upholding the Gandhian principles. The play ends symbolically with Ahmed confirming his stand of pursuing his Marxist revolution, while Prof. Datta's wife observing Ahmed, picks up healthy rice seeds from a tray and flings into fertile soil. The play pictures the futility of Marxist ideology bringing destruction through revolution.

The Refugee is a drama of social realism portraying the misery of the Bangladesh refugees in the 1970s. The story revolves around Yassin, a refugee from East Pakistan who gets involved in the liberation of his land joining Mukti Bahini, coming to Bengal as a refugee Yassin is given shelter by Sengupta who was himself a refugee. Inspired by Sengupta's children Mita and Ashok, Yassin takes up the challenge to liberate his people.

The play is a superb analysis of the human predicament that the central characters face in the wake of the refugee crisis in Bengal. More than the refugee-rehabilitation programme, the play portrays the ideological conflict in the various characters who are caught up between the forces of nationalism and humanism. Finally Yassin plunges into action setting aside his non-committal attitude.

Sonar Bangla is built around external and internal conflicts. External conflicts consist of those between East and West Pakistan, Hindus and Muslims in East Pakistan, Bengali Muslims and guerillas. All this in the backdrop of the refugee crisis leads to Indo-Pak war and the emergence of Bangaladesh. The internal conflict is shown through characters like Hussain and Mujib. When the war breaks out Hussain articulates his fears.

The various places Currimbhoy visited became sources for his plays. During the second period of his literary career, Currimbhoy got more serious regarding his dramatic art. In 1969 which was the Gandhi centenary year, he wrote *An Experiment With Truth* which covers the whole life of Gandhi. While he was staying in Calcutta, he witnessed the revolt of the Naxals and wrote *Inquilab* which deals with the Naxalite movement. He was inspired to write *Darjeeling Tea?* After his tour in the tea gardens in the hill station of Darjeeling.

The major socio economic changes which Currimbhoy witnessed got expression in his plays. Such as the influx of the refugees and revolt within the city of Calcutta and Bengal became the theme of the play *The Refugee.* The emergence of Bangladesh provoked him to write *Sonar Bangla.* The plight of the rural society during the drought in Maharashtra in the seventies formed the background for *The Miracle Seed.*

The Dissident MLA is about the riots in Gujrat which resulted in the abolition of the Assembly in 1974. The last play from Currimbhoy was *This Alien...Native Land* based on the identity crisis of Jews. From his plays, it can be easily understood that Currimbhoy believes in depicting what he perceives in his surroundings. He has his own individual views on the art of drama. He is a dramatist with social purpose. This is made clear when he says that he is a writer of plays which have a certain amount of meaning.

The fact that what he write is socially directed in an environment to which it has pertinence of relevance does put me into the classification of being a writer with a social purpose. He has his own views on dramatic art. For him, there should be a proper blending of artistic and social concerns of dramatists.

Moreover, Currimbhoy considers conflict as the basis of life as well as theatre. Regarding the dramatic language, Indian theatre in English has not grown much in the last generation as we always seem to be borrowing English language plays from the west either in original or suitably adapted. The purpose of a playwright should be the perfect merging of theatre with life so that people could relate themselves with the situation they are watching on the stage.

Currimbhoy is a prolific playwright with social purpose. He has taken up unusual themes from contemporary Indian society and showed his excellence in dramatic art. He wrote more than thirty plays of varied themes regarding social, political and religious problems of contemporary India. The contribution of all the male playwrights is significant in the initial development of Indian drama in English.

His contribution to Indian drama in English is great. His plays show intense realism, but are not literal minded transcription of near facts. We can call his plays as microcosm of Indian life. He seeks to expose his 'vision of man' through his dramatic art. His plays show his abiding faith in the efficacy of love and compassion. His plays serve as panacea to the ills of society. He shows great concern for overall humanity.

5. RABINDRANATH TAGORE

Rabindranath Tagore was born on 6th May 1861. Tagore was born at Dwarkanath Tagore Lane, Jarasanko. He was the son of Debendranath Tagore and Sarada Devi. He was the youngest of fourteen children. As a child, Tagore lived amidst an atmosphere where literary magazines were published, musical recitals were held and theatre performed.

Tagore's oldest brother, Dwijendernath was a respected philosopher and poet. Another brother, Satyendranath was the first ethnically Indian member appointed to the elite and formerly Indian Civil Service. Yet another brother Jyotirindranath was a talented musician, composer and playwright. His sister Swarnakumari Devi earned fame as novelist in her own right. His sister-in-law Kadambari, was a dear friend and has a powerful influence on Tagore.

In early October 1878, Tagore travelled to England with the intent of becoming a barrister. On 10thNovember 1912, Tagore travelled to United States. In the same year, Tagore also travelled the United Kingdom. His International travels sharpened his opinion that human divisions were shallow. The school named Visva-Bharati was founded on 22nd Dec. 1921at Shantiniketan, a spread of relatively arid and eroded red soil of seven acres bought in the 1860s by Debendranth.

Rabindranath Tagore is a towering figure in the millennium-old literature of Bengal. His poetry as well as his novels, short stories and essays are very widely read and the songs he composed are listened with very much interest.

The second half of the nineteenth century is known as the Bankim era of the Bengali literature. The first half of the twentieth century is known as the era of Rabindranath Tagore. His era started with the publication of his poetical works, novels, plays and essays which stamped him as a genius. When he was in the full swing of his career as a writer, he impressed the social and historical movements also.

The British Government has been planning to divide Bengal into two administrative sectors. In 1905, Lord Curzon partitioned Bengal and the Swadeshi Movement started. The artists, poets and dramatists took part in the movement under the leadership of Rabindranath. The restless social, political life impressed all the fields of nation; literature was not the exception for it.

The sensitive writer and person like Rabindranath Tagore could not live away from all these impressions. The reflections of the social and political condition can be found in his all the writings. The Freedom Movement of India did not just remain the political weapon but it tried to bring about revolutionary change in the traditional Indian culture and philosophy.

Ostensibly there are several Tagore-a poet, a novelist, a story writer per excellence, an essayist, a painter, a composer, a philosopher, an educationist a seer. In the present context we bring to the to accentuate Tagore- the playwright, the producer, song writer, musician, the actor, choreographer and stage doer and costume designer and even as a theatre audience.

The towering personality of Rabindranath Tagore also enriched the Bengali drama. His plays were obscure and less stage worthy. But a group of brilliant young graduates staged many of his plays. Sarat Chandra Chatterjee, the famous novelist also tried his hand at drama by writing two plays. Bankim Chatterjee, Nirupama Debi, Sourindra Mohan Mukhopadhya and Majori Bose have some fine plays to their credit.

Rabindranath Tagore's plays were quite distinct from the main body of Bengali drama. He has a distinct place as dramatist. In his plays, Tagore's poetry has tended to overshadow his work. As the outstanding dramaturge of modern India, he has successfully blended the elements of the folk drama of Bengal with classical Sanskrit drama.

Rabindranath wrote over sixty dramas many of which may or may not be called dramas. His range varies from profound tragedies, tragi-comedies, symbolical dramas, allegories, dramas dealing with contemporary social and political problems, dramatic dialogues in verse, lyrical dramas, musical dramas, dance dramas to warm hearted comedies and satires.

Tagore's plays are broadly classified into eight genres as: Musical drama, verse drama, poetic drama, prose drama, comedies, symbolic drama, nature drama and dance drama.

His musical dramas are *Valmiki Pratibha* (The Genius of Valmiki) 1881; *Kal Mrigaya* (The Fateful Hunt) 1882; *Mayar Khela* (The Plays of Illusion) 1888. His verse dramas include *Rudrachanda* 1881, *Prakritir Pratishodh* (Nature's Revenge) 1884, *Raja O Rani* (The King and the Queen), 1880, *Visarjan* (Sacrifice) 1890. Poetic dramas encompass *Chitrangada* 1892, *Viday-Abhishap* (The Curse at Farewell) 1894, *Malini* 1896, *Gandharir Abedan* (Gandhari's Prayer) 1897, *Sati* (The Fateful Wife) 1897, *Karna-Kunti Samvad* (Karna and Kunti Dialogue) 1899, *Lakshmir- Pariksha* (Lakshmi's Testing), 1897.

His prose dramas are *Grihaprabesh* (Homewarming), 1925, *Shodhbodh* (Acquittance), 1926, Natir Puja (The Dancing Girl's Worship) 1926, Tapati, 1929, *Kaler yatra* (The March of Time), 1932, *Chandalika* (The untouchable maid) 1933, *Tasher Desh* (The land of cards) 1933, and *Bansari* 1933.

Under the head 'comedies' fall *Hasyakautuk* (Laughter and fun) 1907, *Vyangyakautuk*(Mockery and Fun) 1907. *Goday Galad* (Wrong from the start) 1892, *Shesh Raksha* (Saved in the End) 1928, *Vaikunther Khata* (The Manuscript of Vaikuntha) 1897, *Bashikaran* (Captivation) 1926 and Muktir Upay (The way to Deliverance), 1938.

Symbolic dramas include *Sharadostav* (Autumn Festival) *Rinsodh* (Repayment of Debt) 1921, *Mukut* (The Crown) 1908, Prayaschitta (Expiation) 1909, *Paritran* (Deliverence) 1929, Raja (The King) 1910, *Arup Ratan* (The Jewel without Form) 1920, *Achalayatan* (The Jewel without Form) 1920, *Achalayatan* (The Static Institution) 1912, *Guru* (The Great Teacher) 1918, *Dakghar* (The Post Office) 1912, *Phagluni* (The cyle of spring) 1916, *Mukta Dhara* (The Free Currence) 1922 and *Raktakarabi* (Red Oleanders) 1924.

Under the division 'Nature Drama' Comes *Vasanta* (The Spring) 1923, *Shesh Varshan* (The Last Rains) 1925, *Shravangatha* (The Song of the Rains) 1934, *Nataraja*:*Riturangashala* (King of Dancers:The Theatre of the Seasons) 1924 and *Navin* (Rejuvenescene) 1930.

Tagore's Dance dramas cover *Shapmochan* (Release from Curse) 1931, *Nrityanatya Chitrangada* 1936, *Chandalika* (The Untouchable Maid) 1938, *Nrityanatya Mayar Khela* 1938-39 and *Shyama* 1939.

Not only dramas but his stories and novels have been copiously dramatized for the stage and many of his poems are presented in the form of dance-drama. Cambridge guide to Theatre holds Tagore as India's best known modern playwright. Although his many plays are not frequently produced outside Bengal, they constitute an important contribution to dramatic literature.

Most of Tagore's dramas are written in winter. He used poetic tools in his dramas. His prose dramas are also having the quality of lyric poetry. His plays achieved a kind of lyrical action and a rhythomic treatment of emotions which moved around one idea. The main principle of his plays is the play of feeling and root of action. Tagore was impressed more with music than action and more with idea than story.

When his *Valmiki Pratibha* was staged Tagore was twenty from that time on, Tagore independently wrote and staged his dramas which were different from Bengali drama.

1. Musical Drama

Tagore's musical dramas are *Valmiki Pratibha, Kal Mrigaya* and *Mayar khela.* These three plays were the innovative musical genre, the work of a young musician-dramatist, a specialist artist, marked the emergence of a new force in the world of Bengali drama. These plays exhibit a daring integration of drama and music where the dramatist freely melodising native and foreign tunes established a highly effective dramatic form on the stage. These three plays are operatic and are different from Bengali *Gitabhinay* and Marathi *Sangit Natak* in conception.

2. Verse Drama

Rudrachanda, Prakritir Pratisodh, Raja O Rani and *Visarjan* have a complicated ground of action, mixture of verse and prose. Songs from enhancing the intensity of dramatic moments; comic relief is presented in the last three plays, revenge as a motif. These are having focus on the 'emotional life of the characters'; soliloquy and an exception in Indian drama, exhibition of death on stage. *Rudra Chanda* (1881) has a revenge theme.

3. Poetic Drama

In his poetic dramas Tagore uses the literary haritages such as *the Mahabharata, the Buddhist legend, the Maratha ballad* and *Folklore.* He used the *Mahabharata* for his *Chitrangada, Viday Abhishap, Gandharir Abedan, Narakbas, Karna-Kunti-sambad. The Buddhist Legend* for his play *Malini. The Maratha Ballad* for *Sati* and *folklore* for *Lakhsmir Parisksha.*

4. Comedies

Tagore's comedies are fresh and forever they will remain fresh. The wit, humour presented in his plays, sketches is intensely enjoyable. Rabindranath wrote a couple of comedies *Goday Golad* and *Vaikunther Katha.* His comic muse effectively expresses itself in those plays. Those are highly performable plays that accord with the norms of high comedy. It shows the dexterity of the artist in handling theme, form technique and tense.

5. Prose Drama

In his prose dramas *Girth Pravesh, Shodhbodh* and *Banshari* are written in a contemporary setting. *Natir Puja* and *Chandalika* are legend based, *Tapati* and *Paritran* are semi historical, *Rather Rashi* and *Kabir Diksha* are apocatyptic and *Tasher Desh* is a dramatic fantasy.

6. Symbolic Drama

Tagore's symbolic plays are *Shardotsav* (1908), *Mukut*(1908), *Prayaschitta*(1909), *Raja*(1910), *Achalayatan* (1912), *Dakghar*(1912), *Phalguni*(1916), *Muktadhara*(1922), *Raktakarabi*(1924) and the revised versions such as *Aruprtan*(1920), *Guru*(1918), *Rinsodh* (1921) and *Paritran* (1929).

7. Nature Drama

Tagore himself has called 'Ritu Utsav' (Season festivals) to his nature drama. Nature drama is more befetting a designation, considering their cosmic scope. In these drama nature is viewed through the prismatic appearance of the seasons in their eternal cycle includes corresponding changes in all that come within their grand sweep.

His nature dramas or season plays are *Basanta* (The Spring) 1923, *Shesh Varshan* (The Last Rain) 1925, *Shravangatha* (The Song of the Rains) 1934, *Nataraj:Riturangashala* (King of Dancers : The Theatre of the seasons) 1927, *Nabin* (Rajuvenescence) 1930.

8. Dance Drama

His dance dramas include *Shapmochan* (Release from curse) 1931, *Nrityanatya Chitrangada*(1936), *Chandalika* (The Untouchable Maid) 1938, *Nrityanatya Mayarkhela*(1938-39) and *Shayma* (1939).

Stage

Most of the Tagore plays were intended to be played in the open air or on open air stages with the minimum of stage properties. No cut or painted scenes were allowed. In the formative stage of the Tagore theatre, the poet himself was his own producer, director, designer and dresser.

Costume

Rabindranath invariably gave great importance to the stage costume. Probably he realised that it is possible for the theatre to do without stage, but acting must mean 'assuming a character', and assuming a character means dressing up.

Music

In the domain of music, Tagore built up the edifice that has now come to be known as 'Rabindra Sangit', a new genre in *artha sangit*. Some of his tunes are improvements on the metre, being lightened and quickened by the addition of the musical beat.

The tunes and melodies created by Tagore have an unspeakable charm which comes from the moulding of the music pattern that the tune follows a rhythm of its own, a rhythm that combines in itself the metrical, musical and dance beats.

His music sometimes sounds like rhythmic chanting. Rabindranath, has successfully conceived a musical style which emphasises and achieves an artistically satisfying blending of words and melody.

Dance

The credit of introducing original dance drams to the elite of the city goes to Tagore. He was strongly under the spell of Manipuri dance form and employed the style into his dance creations. The abhinaya part of part of his dance is borrowed from Kathakali. This mixed style of form is often termed as Rabindrik style of dance. His dance dramas found an adequate expression not only in just words and musical compositions but dance played as equally vital role. As a dance-director he used to edit the dancing while rehearsal was in progress.

Actor

Tagore was only sixteen when he made his first appearance on the stage. This was a comedy by Jyotrindranath with Rabindranth in the leading role. He also acted in his own plays *Valmiki Pratibha, Kal Marigaya, Visarjan, Chirkumarsabha, Phalguni, Tapati, Natir Puja* etc.

Tagore's characterization of Valmiki established him as a gifted actor and a fashionable stage vocalist. He acted in his *Phalguni.* He played the role of the blind minstrel with confidence. The impressive presence of Tagore on the stage in diverse roles thereafter added fresh dimension to their conception leaving an indelible mark on the audience.

From then on, when he was twenty one he directed, produced and acted in many of the forty odd plays long and short, of his own. He was seventy five when he last appeared in *Sharadostav* staged in 1935 at Santiniketan. Tagore easily achieved that celtimate goal of all good actors that is identifying oneself with the role portrayed.

Rabindranath was against the unrestrained exaggeration in acting, which according to him completely spoils the clarity and inner beauty of the play. Tagore had not spared the English actors, the distant idols of the Bengali theatre of those days. He attended the world famous *Passion play* in Oberammergau at Munich.

Rabindranath's *Raja O Rani* was first staged at the Emerald Theatre in 1890. Since then, his early dramas and comedies were presented intermittently at various public theatres. Out of his sixty dramas only fifteen were performed in his life time.

Of his great symbolic plays only one performance took place in his life time. In composition and in production the works of Tagore were far superior to anything that had been done before the stage history of Bengal. Thus, Rabindranath Tagore was the man, greater than work. He has a multidimensional qualities and a versatile genius.

His plays are technically like folk plays and Sanskrit plays. He makes use of myths, legends, symbol, allegory, songs and dialogues. Tagore shows originality in the technique of his plays.

Tagore's *Achalayatan* is an allegorical play inspired from Rajendralal Mitra's '*Sanskrit Budhist Literature of Nepal*'. He completed the play in 1911. It was first appeared in the journal '*Prabasi*'. It was published in book form for the first time in 1912. The play was dedicated to Sri Jadunath Sarkar. It can be regarded as an allogerical play, an attempt to repudiate our absurd Hindoo orthodoxies, our meaning and antiquated socio-religious rites, belief and taboos.

His *Ama and Vinayaka* is based on a short verse play '*Sati*' written in 1899. '*Sati*' was publihsed in *Kahini*. It presents Rabindranath's conception of religion. His *Arasiker Svargaprapti,*is a comic playlet appeared in 1892. It is primarily in the form of monologue. Mythological material is comically used in this playlet.

His *Arupratan* is a symbolic play. It is a revised version of '*Raja*'. It appeared in 1920. It is an actable shortened version of Raja-rewritten in a new form. Tagore's *Autumn Festival* is based on Bengali original *Sharadostav*. It is his first season drama written for the young boys at Santiniketan without any female character.

It is a prose play interspersed with songs. It is a symbolic drama. His *Banshari* is a tragi-comedy, published in 1933. It is based on his novelette *Lalater Likhan*. It was never played on the stage. It dramatizes the emancipation from the bondage of the passion of self-gratifying love to the condition of dispassionate love.

The lyrical drama of Tagore *Chitrangada* is almost perfect in unity and conception, magical in expression, a nearly flawless whole, knit together by the glowing heat of inspiration. Inevitably, *Chitrangada* is a love story but a moral is woven into the texture of the play. Chitra lives by its sensuous poetry, not its dry morality.

Traditional cultures have their own tension but this tear filled spring will outlast the philosophy of self-control. Indeed the theme is the enchantment of spring and the power of its spell on the senses. Chitra, entitled after her name goes to win the love of Arjuna in the forest temple of Shiva but is disappointed.

Chitra understands that her physical beauty cannot win his love and decides to win it by making it spiritual. In the play *Chitra*, we have not the same effluence of mystical thought and emotion as in other plays .But we have in it a realization of the diviner element of love and life, a heavenly message to the human soul as to what is the meaning of love in the truest sense of the term.

In the play *The King And The Queen*, king Vikram is totally attracted towards the physical charm of his queen Sumitra, the infatuated king neglects his royal duties towards the state. The theme of love in it is shown in a wider sense. He asks her to leave the house and its service alone, because his heart cannot spare her. Thus the husband, being an infatuated lover looses the wife's respect and the confidence with which he vindicates his manhood.

He is so passionately in love with her that he spends his time hovering round her. Taking advantage of his infatuation for the queen, her relatives from Kashmir manage to grab all important position in the state and fatten on their spoils. Complaints reached to the king but he has no ear and has no time to waste over vulgar concerns when life is short and love so sweet. Thus Tagore expresses the sensation both gay and melancholic under the dominating emotions of love and its allied sentiments.

The transient psychological states under the stress of love, restlessness and curiosity are described with a highly developed sense of physical perception and intuitive awareness. *Red Oleander*'s Nandini in a fervently rhetorical speech, proclaim her pious and joyful attachment with Ranjan, who for her is a personification of beauty and youth.

Tagore's plays deal with the mystery of human existence. His plays are theme oriented and symbolical. His themes are varied and the treatment is also varied and well suited to the theme. His plays are expressions of the problems of human life. He raises some problem or other in his plays and often his solution does not appeal to the reader. He highlights how love, religion and death can be life giving forces.

6. VIJAY TENDULKAR

Vijay Tendulkar, one of the outstanding Indian playwrights, was born in Mumbai on 6th January 1928 in a Bhalawalikar Saraswat Brahmin family in Kolhapur, Maharashtra. He spent his early childhood in Bombay. There was a literature friendly atmosphere in his family. In addition to holding a clerical job, his father also ran a small publishing business.

He was an amateur actor and director as well. The house was full of books and his father encouraged him to read. The literary environment at home and his interaction with books and writers at his father's shop inspired young Vijay to take up to writing. He at the age six he wrote his first story.

When Vijay Tendulkar was a child he was living in Bombay. He witnessed the communal riots from his balcony. He saw the incidents of stabbing. As a child he found difficult to understand death and suffering, but spectacles implant deep impact on him. His father, Dhondopant, was Head-Clerk at Longmans, Green and Company, a British publishing firm.

He had been invited to join a professional theatre company but he refused because a career in the theatre was not considered respectable. Every Sunday morning his father takes Vijay to the large bookshop owned by his publisher friend. So the books in the house and outside had become young Vijay's favourite friends and companions.

At age eleven, he wrote, directed, and acted in his first play. At age of fourteen he participates in the 1942 Indian freedom movement, and leaves his studies.

Tendulkar worked as a proof-reader in various printing presses from 1944 to 1947. Then Tendulkar started his career writing for newspapers and magazines. In 1948, he worked as sub-editor in daily 'Navabharat'. He also worked for 'Maratha' and 'Loksatta'. He was the executive editor of magazines 'Vasudha' and 'Dipawali' for some time. He wrote columns for 'Manus' and 'Maharashtra Times'. He also worked as a public relations officer for the Chowgule Group of Industries.

During his career as a journalist, he got an exhaustive knowledge of society and human life. His varied professional experience brought him in touch with people of all classes. While working for daily 'Maratha', he came into contact with Acharya Atre, an eminent Marathi playwright. Atre`s guidance had a significant impact on Tendulkar`s writing. Tendulkar's journalistic background sharpens his objective and narrative style of writing.

Vijay Tendulkar' was a leading Indian playwright, movie and television writer, literary essayist, political journalist, and social commentator. He mostly writes in Marathi language but his plays translated in so many international languages. He is most known for his plays, 'Shantata! Court Chalu Ahe', 'Ghashiram Kotwal', 'Sakharam Binder', Kamala, Gidhade and other.

He won Maharashtra State government awards in 1956, 1969 and 1972; and "Maharashtra Gaurav Puraskar" in 1999. He was honored with the Sangeet Natak Akademi Award in 1970, and again in 1998 with the Academy's highest award for 'lifetime-contribution', the Sangeet Natak Akademi Fellowship (Ratna Sadasya). In 1984, he received the Padma Bhushan award from the Government of India for his literary accomplishments.

In 1977, Tendulkar won the National Film Award for Best Screenplay for his screenplay in Shyam Benegal's movie, Manthan (1976). He has written screenplays for some of the important art movies of India, such as Nishant,

Aakrosh and Ardha Satya. For the past five decades, Tendulkar has been a highly influential dramatist and theatre personality in Maharashtra.

Vijay Tendulkar can be acknowledged as the precursor of modern Indian drama. His contribution is marvelous and bulky in the development of modern dramatic sensibility. Though he did write much more in Marathi, the translated work from Marathi to other Indian language is really mind blowing.

His plays were translated in English as well as more than ten international languages. His plays were performed internationally in different languages. He was born in Kolhapur and grown up in a ritualistic Brahmin family; he began to write when he was only six years old. He didn't believe in idealism as his many plays derived inspiration from real life incidents or social upheavals which provides clear light on harsh realities.

Tendulkar's play *Kamla* was inspired by a real life incident published in the *Indian Express.* A person called Ashwin Sarin, actually bought a girl from a rural flesh market and presented at a press conference. Using this incident as a launching pad, Tendulkar has raised certain value system of modern, success oriented generation who are ready to sacrifice human values in the name of humanity itself.

The central character of the play is a self-seeking journalist, Jai Singh Jadhav, who treats the woman he has purchased from the flesh market as a object that can procure from him a promotion in his job and a refutation in his professional life. Jai Singh buys, Kamla, an Adivasi woman, at the flesh market of Luhardaya beyond Ranchi for two hundred and fifty rupees. Jai Singh's enthusiasm is directed towards sheer sensationalism.

He creates sensationalism at the express of Kamla. He sells a woman that poor and illiterate woman. Jai Singh Jadhav discards Kamla is an orphanage for woman and washes off his hands for his safety, after she ceases to be an advantage to him. Jai Singh Jadhav exploits not only Kamla but also his wife, Sarita. It is through Sarita, Tendulkar exposes the Chauvinism intrinsic in the modern male who believes himself to be liberal minded.

Jai Singh- through his treatment of Kamla, makes Sarita realize that she is also a slave a lovely bonded labourer to him. She observes how he refuses a bath to Kamla and takes her in clumsy clothes to the press-conference for his professional profit. Jai Singh uses both the woman, Kamla and Sarita as pawns in his game of chess. Jai Singh the Persecutor, persecutes his victims- Kamala, Sarita and Kamala bai.

Tendulkar wrote the play, *Shāntatā! Court Chālu Aahe* (*Silence! The Court Is In Session*). It was presented on the stage for the first time in 1967, and proved as one of his finest works. Satyadev Dubey presented it in movie form in 1971 with Tendulkar's collaboration as the screenplay writer. *Silence! The Court Is In Session* by playwright Vijay Tendulkar, was originally written in Marathi as "*Shāntatā! Court Chālu Aahe*".

It was staged for the first time in 1967, and has been translated into several languages and adapted by various theatre troupes over the years. The play is a social satire on middle-class society, particularly its treatment of women. The play consists of middle-class characters.

In *Silence! The Court is in Session*, Tendulkar has depicted the plight of a young woman, who is betrayed by the male dominated society. A traditional male dominated society cannot relinquish its paralyzed values and customs. The society does not like to perceive or receive any social change. Tendulkar presents a treatment of those ugly ways of society in this play.

Tendulkar has criticized the middle-class morality that throttles the tender desires of Benare, a middle class woman, to mother a child in the play. Tendulkar seems to leave the play without suggesting any solution to the problem. None in the play is ready to sympathize with Benare.

Only Mr. Kashikar, the judge, feels that they are going too far in their mock-trial but, then, he immediately silences his conscience. After all the Court is in session and everyone is expected to keep silence! Tendulkar covertly pleads for sympathy for the victims of the society through this flash of humanity for a moment in the heart of Mr. Kashikar

In his 1972 play, *Sakharam Binder* (Sakharam, the Binder), Tendulkar dealt with the topic of domination of the male gender over the female gender. As the title suggests, the play revolves around Sakharam and his curious life-style. Sakharam, is a man devoid of ethics and morality, and professes not to believe in outdated social codes and conventional marriage.

The play's main conflict is set in motion when Laxmi returns after Sakharam sent her packing, and convinces Champa to let her stay. It is not the plot, however, but the depth and the subtlety of Bernard White's portrayal of Sakharam that injects variety, surprise and fascination into this almost three-hour play.

Mr. White vividly captures the strange and complex pathology of Sakharam, who seems to want to please his "birds" even as he bullies them and who speaks like a freethinking crusader for women's rights one minute and like a philistine scornful of their devotion to him the next. Sakharam's tragedy turns out to hinge on his budding social consciousness, his arrested enlightenment.

Kanyadaan by Vijay Tendulkar studies a case of spousal abuse and interrogates many of the issues mentioned above concerning this domestic problem and reasons why victims and their relatives allow it to continue. The play deals with a wife who begins by ignoring or explaining away obvious signals that her fiancé would be a wife-beater, marries him in spite of her observations, leaves him when he assaults her, but returns when he comes pleading.

She then sticks by him amid sustained brutalization, allows him to exploit her, refuses the help of her family and even exiles herself from them. But the play's treatment further complicates a complex issue, doing more than highlighting a social ill, as theatre is wont to do. It dramatizes a house divided against itself, a vivid case of gender politics, national politics, ideology and tradition.

Tendulkar proved himself as talented writer who has great faith in his passion. His humanistic and fearless attitude becomes apparent from his literature as well as his social work. His writing never hesitated while expressing his own views. Tendulkar belonged to the middle class and depicted the assessment and problems, hopes and misery, in the life of the middle class society effectively.

Tendulkar has written twenty-five one-act-plays, thirty full-length plays, two novels, a biography, five collection of short stories, sixteen plays for children and five volumes of literary essays and social criticism. His columns in news papers like 'Kovali Unhe' and 'Ram Prahar' became popular.

He has translated nine novels, two biographies and five plays by other authors into Marathi. In 1990s he wrote an acclaimed television series 'Swayamsiddha'. He has written screenplays for twelve movies in Hindi and eight movies in Marathi.

We can say that Indian literature is fortunate enough to produce a versatile genius like Vijay Tendulkar whose contribution is remarkable not only in the development of the Indian drama but also lies in providing proper name and magnitude to Modern Indian drama.

Tendulkar's plays are unconventional and he penetrated the dark corners, the repression, the brutality, rejection and alienation of his characters. According to him to break the traditional framework of the Marathi theatre was essential and to do some experiment with the theatre was necessary. This view of Tendulkar shows that he was influenced by a French dramatist Antonin Artaud who replaced the French "bourgeois" classical theatre with the "theatre of cruelty" and in his plays he liberated the human subconscious and revealed man to himself.

Tendulkar's Gidhade perhaps was influenced by Artaud's 'Theatre of Cruelty' and he wanted to do experiment with it. The Indian culture has a spiritual base. We are God fearing people who believe in virtue or sin. Thus there is cultural restraint. Traditional, moral and spiritual values have taught us tolerance, respect, sexual self control and self sacrifice when necessary. Insecurity due to economic conditions, communal stratification, and caste system does not allow much freedom to the individual. Individual freedom does not have much scope in our social set up.

7. SRI AUROBINDO

Aurobindo was born in a westernized doctor's family who tried to protect his children from the ill-effects of Hinduism and Indian manners. Dr. Krishnadhan Ghosh sent his children away from India to England for education. Aurobindo was only seven years old. Totally away from Indian Atmosphere, he studied there anglicized manners.

He intentionally missed the riding test of Indian Civil Service examination though he had good score in exam and got disqualified. He joined some secret societies in England which were fighting for Indian freedom. He made his participation open in the nationalist movement leaving Baroda service.

In 1910, Aurobindo actively participated in the Indian freedom struggle. With Bal Gangadhar Tilak as the leader of the extremist group in Congress, Aurobindo demanded complete freedom. During this period, he wrote extensively in Bande Mataram and other nationalist journals inflaming Indians with ideas of fight for freedom.

Nationalist politics landed him in jail in 1909 in Alipore bombing case. After acquittal, he went to Pondicherry and founded there an ashram to preach nationalism and spiritualism till his death.

Sri Aurobindo (1872-1950) was also a major Indian English playwright. During 1891-1916, he wrote five complete and six incomplete verse plays. One of the most interesting features of his plays is the variety of periods and places. The two major themes of his plays are the idea of human evolution and love. The famous plays are *Perseus the Deliverer, The Viziers of Bassora, Prince of Edur, Eric, Vavadutta* and *Savitri*. Sri Aurobindo employs ancient legends to highlight the contemporary urge for freedom and bondage and heighten the elements of heroism, adventure and mystery in the actions of his imaginary characters and as such, all his plays are imbued with a strong romantic impulse which appears to be the driving force behind all his plays.

In spite of his vast learning, he seems to have overlooked the rich tradition of Indian drama especially dramatic techniques. In order to express his romantic impulse, he has focused largely on the models of Elizabethan Drama. His plays are either in verse or a mixture of prose and verse. At times, he shows his ability in composing realistic dialogues in colloquial English. Regarding themes, he does not confine himself to one particular country and locales.

In *Perseus the Deliverer* the grand poetry of the prologue is immediately followed by banter in prose in Act 1 Scene I. The mighty world of the Gods and their cosmic struggle is presented in the prologue in reverberating poetry. The next scene brings us down to the familiar work-a-day world of Syria with the witty Diomede and matter-of-fact Cireas exchanging views about work, weather and palace gossip.

Characters can be prosaic or poetic and they carry the necessary vibrations into the atmosphere. At Bagdad, the highly poetic and romantic exchange of lovers is interrupted by Ibrahim who is the most prosaic and earthly character in *The Viziers of Bassora*.

Once Ibrahim enters, Nureddene and Anice Aljalice who have been speaking verse switch over to prose, but the minute Ibrahim leaves to fetch wine, the lovers swing back to verse. Andromeda in *Perseus the Deliverer* has a poetic aura about her and its impact is felt the moment she makes her entry. Diomede who has been discussing palace news with Praxilla in prose, suddenly breaks into poetry as she sees Andromeda walking into the room.

The moment Andromeda makes her exit, the dialogue loses its elevation and comes down to the plane of prose. This shift is also maintained in his *The Hero and the Nymph* which is a translation of Kalidasa's Vikramorvasie. Manavaka, the King's jester speaks verse with the king but in his exchanges with Nipunka the queen's maid, he speaks prose.

In *The Prince of Edur* all the girls in the women's apartment of Edur's palace are pelting wit in prose and the target is the prospective suitor for Comol's hand. Just then the message about trip to Dongurh is conveyed and Comol suddenly switches over to poetry. The change immediately suggests to us that the pastoral Dongurh is a suitable place for love and romance. We no longer worry about the safety of the princess.

Cireas in *Perseus the Deliverer* speaks prose in all the scenes except one. During the course of a crisp prose dialogue with Diomede, he suddenly shifts to poetry on seeing the 'Phoenician Galley' caught in surf. He finds the scene of shipwreck truly magnificent and so will it be to a product of a barbaric civilization.

Prose is the natural idiom of the comic characters of lowlife like Harkoos and Kareem in *Viziers of Bassora*. The language of these characters reveals their realistic and amoral attitude to life. Nuredenne is facing a financial crisis and his servant Harkoos comes back with the report that all his master's "friends" have failed him. One friend Ghaneem "Has broken his leg for the present and cannot see anyone for a long fortnight". Another "has gone into the country—upstairs".

Of yet another he says, "Every time I mentioned money, he drowned the subject in tears" (*CP* 645). Kareem the fisherman is, likewise matter of fact in his speech. The great Caliph Haroun Al Rasheed who wants to go disguised, exchanges his royal robes for Kareem's filthy gabardine.

But in other plays including the fragments the dramatic prose is used by Sri Aurobindo with remarkable dexterity to suit the requirements of mood, character or situation. The alternate use of prose and verse serves to establish dramatic contrast. It contrasts the gross world from the grand one, the frivolous world from the world of high seriousness. And it certainly contrasts earthly characters from the elevated ones.

Sri Aurobindo's wielding of prose and verse with equal ease no doubt shows him a master of language to whose touch both modes are equally pliant. But what is more significant is the fact that it brings out his caliber as a poetic dramatist-a dramatist who can trace the inner workings of a character in a given situation through the medium of language.

8. CONCLUSION

Drama is the prominent form of literature. Its success depends more on the performance than on its written counterpart. It articulates message for the viewers largely through its stage performance, marked by its distinctiveness like pluralism and dynamism. It breaks the web of illusion and developing understanding and perception of the people.

Drama being an audiovisual medium of expression has been a very effective and powerful genre in world literature. The birth and development of drama in Greece, Rome, England and India emphasizes upon the fact that it has always been an essential part of culture, highlighting and evaluating ethical commitments, religious convictions, philosophical approaches, and social and political changes in various countries.

Hailed as the "Fifth Veda" drama in India has had a rich and magnificent tradition. The origin of Indian drama can thus be traced back to the Vedic period. It is believed that the dramatic tradition of the ancient Hindus was fully developed even before the Greek drama came to their knowledge.

Indian-English Drama saw the first light of the day when Krishna Mohan Banerjee wrote "The Persecuted" in 1813. The postmodern era seems to be productive for Indian English Drama as it has received fresh momentum from young writers like Mahesh Dattani and Manjula Padmanabhan. R.K. Dhawan rightly observes that Very recently Indian English Drama has shot into importance.

Younger writers like Mahesh Dattani and Manjula Padmanabhan have infused new life into this branch of writing. Both Dattani and Padmanabhan project stark realism through their plays. The scarcity of Indian Drama in

English is credited to some reasons, the first and the foremost being the want of a living theatre.

Drama is meant to be staged. The role of the audience is an important factor in the success of a stage show. The study of drama is half literary and half sociological because drama comes in direct contact with the masses, literate as well as illiterate, through, stage production.

The stunted growth of Indian-English Drama is also due to the incapability of Indian playwrights in English to draw upon the rich and varied Indian dramatic traditions and make use of the rich over abundance of Indian myth and Indian historical heritage. However the major obstacle and set back in the development of Indian-English Drama is language. Natural conversation is the most important aspect of drama but when two Indian

Indian English drama beyond the limitations of imitation, amateur, translations, and proper patronage has immersed as a potent one to make a representation of the dilemmas of human existence expressed in terms of gender inequalities, caste ridden practices, social discrimination and all pervasive moral depravity deriving strength from its structural compactness and ability to bridge up direct communication between the sensitive soul of the artist and the audience.

The Indian dramatists are reflecting upon the issues that beset human race for a long. The 20th century witnessed radical and rapid changes and alteration in number of fields of human interests and investments. There has also occurred a radical and rapid shift of values and notions. It demanded urgent need to address the shifting values and notions in our society. Stirred by this situation, the dramatists of our time grabbed the opportunity of addressing the pains and misery, suffering and subjugation of the unreached and unprivileged sections of our society.

Drama is perhaps the most touching medium of representation of human life. It has power to surface the conscience of the audience. What is very essential is the active participation of the audience. The dramatic experience is like touching a bare electric wire. The drama, being dynamic medium, depicts the dynamics of human experiences acquainting us with character's veiled and intricate pattern of human consciousness.

The need to address human misery and consistent mechanism of humiliation compels the dramatists to deviate from the traditional path and reshape the conventional canons and concepts of stage art and craft capable of creating spaces for registering remonstration against the mortification of humanity as a whole.

Some leading dramatists like Girish Karnad, Badal Sircar, Mohan Rakesh, Vijay Tendulkar and a host of other dramatists have dealt with various issues that have been lashing out human beings for ages. They have mirrored the problems and issues of contemporary Indian society. However, none of them has ever made them as essential part of their dramatic art.

Drama is perhaps the most touching standard of depiction of human life. It has power to surface the conscience of the audience. What is very essential is the active participation of the audience. The dramatic experience is like touching a bare electric wire. The drama, being dynamic medium, depicts the dynamics of human experiences acquainting us with character's indirect and complex pattern of human consciousness.

The need to address human misery and consistent mechanism of humiliation compels the dramatists to diverge from the traditional path and reform the conventional canons and concepts of stage art and craft capable of creating spaces for registering complaint against the mortification of humanity as a whole.

Some leading dramatists like Girish Karnad, Badal Sircar, Mohan Rakesh, Vijay Tendulkar and a host of other dramatists have dealt with various issues that have been lashing out human beings for ages. They have mirrored the problems and issues of contemporary Indian society. However, none of them has ever made them as essential part of their dramatic art.

References

1. A.B. Keith, *The Sanskrit Drama*, Motilal Banarasidas, New Delhi 1992.
2. K.A. Agrawal, *The Best Plays of Asif Currimbhoy*, Jaipur: Book Enclave, 2007.
3. Bandopadhyay and Samik, *Vijay Tendulkar: Collected Plays in Translation*, Mumbai: Oxford University, 2003.
4. Bhatta S. Krishna, *Indian English Drama: A Critical Study*, New Delhi. Sterling Publishers. 1970.75.
5. Diana Devlin, *From Mask and Scene*: *An Introduction to a World View of Theatre*, London, Macmillan, 1989.
6. Dodiya, Jaydipish, Ed. *The Plays of Girish Karnad*, New Delhi: Prestige Books, 1999.
7. Iyengar and K.R. Srinivasa. *Indian Writing in English*. New Delhi: Sterling Publishers Private Limited, 1983.
8. Karnad and Girish, *Three Plays: Naga-Mandala, Hayavadana and Tughlaq*, New Delhi: OUP, 2007.
9. M.K. Naik, *Dimensions of Indian English Literature*, New Delhi: Sterling Publishers, 1984.
10. R.K. Narayan, *The English Teacher*, Indian Thought Publications, Chennai.
11. Reddy P. Bayapa, *The Plays of Asif Currimbhoy*, Writers Workshop Calcutta., 1985.

12. N.M. Sen, *Glorious Thought Of Tagore,* New Delhi: New Books Society of India, 1965.

13. Shukla Supriya, Indian English Drama: An Introduction. *Perspectives and challenges in Indian English drama*, ed. Neeru Tandon, New Delhi. Atlantic publication, 2006. 11..

14. K. V. Surendran, *Indian Literature in English*: New Perspectives, New Delhi: Sarup and Sons, 2002.

15. Tagore, Rabindranath, *Chitrangada*. London, Macmillan And Company Ltd, 1938.

16. Tagore, Rabindranath, *Red Oleanders*. London: Macmillan And Company Ltd, 1938.

17. Tagore, Rabindranath, *The King And The Queen*. London: Macmillan And Company Ltd, 1889.

18. Thompson and Edward, *Rabindranath Tagore: Poet and Dramatist.* New Delhi: oxford University Press, 1994.

19. G.J. Watson, *Drama: An Introduction,* London: The Macmillan press Ltd, 1983.

20. Williams and Raymond, *Drama from Ibsen to Brecht,* Australia: Penguin Books, 1973.

21. Yadav and Saryug, *Indian English Drama*, Ed. Jaydip Singh K. Dodiya. New Delhi, Sarup & Sons, 2010.